LOCAL CHURCH EVANGELISM

LOCAL CHURCH EVANGELISM

Patterns and Approaches

Edited by
David F Wright and Alastair H Gray

THE SAINT ANDREW PRESS: EDINBURGH

First published in 1987 by
THE SAINT ANDREW PRESS
121 George Street, Edinburgh EH2 4YN
in conjunction with the
Research and Publications Committee of
Rutherford House, Claremont Park, Edinburgh

Copyright 1987 |©| Rutherford House, Edinburgh
ISBN 0 7152 0611 7

British Library Cataloguing in Publication Data

Local church evangelism: patterns and
approaches.
1. Evangelistic work
I. Gray, Alastair H. II. Wright, David F.
269'.2   BV3790

ISBN 0-7152-0611-7

*The Publisher acknowledges financial assistance from The Drummond Trust towards the
publication of this volume.*

Scripture quotations marked 'GNB' come from the Good News Bible © American
Bible Society 1976, published by The Bible Societies and Collins. Used by
permission.

Scripture quotations marked 'NIV' are from the Holy Bible, New International
Version. Copyright © 1973, 1978, 1984 International Bible Society. Published by
Hodder & Stoughton.

Extracts from the Authorized King James Version of the Bible, which is Crown
Copyright in the United Kingdom, are reproduced by permission of Eyre &
Spottiswoode (Publishers) Limited, Her Majesty's Printers, London.

Typeset by Print Origination, Formby, Lancs.
Printed by Bell & Bain, Glasgow

Contents

Notes on Contributors   7
Introduction—*David F Wright*   9
The Missionary Parish—*Ian Doyle*   12

I—Evangelism in the Setting of the Congregation
1 Congregational Surveys: Preparation for Evangelism
      —*Lewis Misselbrook*   21
2 House Groups and Church Organisations—*Shirley Fraser*   29
3 Baptisms, Marriages and Funerals—*David Searle*   35
4 Worship and Evangelism—*Jock Stein*   42
5 Bible-Teaching Ministry and Evangelism—*William Still*   50

II—Outreach to the Parish and Community
1 City-Centre Lunch-Hour Services—*Roger Simpson*   55
2 Outreach in the Inner City—*Howard Hudson*   59
3 Mission in a Rural Community—*David Young*   65
4 Personal Evangelism in the Parish—*William Carmichael*   72
5 Church Extension Opportunities—*Ray Sawers*   78
6 Parish-Based Mission—*Dennis Lennon*   84

III—Partnership Between Churches in Mission
1 Presbytery-Wide Mission—*Andrew McGowan*   93
2 Town-Wide Mission—*Robert McGhee*   99
3 Festivals of Faith—*Peter Neilson*   105

IV—Using Outside Resources
1 Training for Evangelism: National Resources for Local
      Mission—*Peter Bisset*   113
2 Using a Student Mission Team—*Peter Humphris*   122
3 College Mission Teams—*Chris Wigglesworth*   126
4 Bible Society Literature for Outreach—*Fergus Macdonald*   130
5 Using a Mission Team—*Stephen Anderson*   136

V—Mission to Young People
1   Young People Outside the Church—*Lance Stone*   143
2   Young People in Church Circles—*Andy Thornton*   149
3   Local Church Involvement in Summer Missions
        —*Douglas Nicol*   154
4   Holiday Clubs for Children—*Mary-Clare Duncan*   161
5   Children Within the Church: An Alternative Approach
        —*Lance Stone*   167
6   Family Services—*Alastair Gray*   171
7   Evangelistic Youth Magazines—*Alastair Gray*   174

Epilogue
The Way Ahead—*Peter Neilson*   179

Notes on Contributors

Captain Stephen Anderson, Church of Scotland Evangelist

The Revd Peter T Bisset, Warden, St Ninian's (Training and Resource Centre), Crieff

The Revd William Carmichael, Minister, Restalrig Church, Edinburgh

The Revd Dr Ian B Doyle, Joint Secretary, Department of Ministry and Mission, Church of Scotland

Miss Mary-Clare Duncan, Schoolteacher, formerly Scripture Union Staff Worker

Miss Shirley Fraser, Social Worker, Holy Trinity Church, Wester Hailes, Edinburgh

The Revd Alastair H Gray, Minister, Garvald and Morham with Haddington West Churches, East Lothian

The Revd Howard R Hudson, Minister, St Francis-in-the-East Church, Glasgow

The Revd Peter M Humphris, Minister, Mains of Fintry Church, Dundee

The Revd Dennis R Lennon, Rector, St Thomas's Episcopal Church, Corstorphine, Edinburgh

The Revd Fergus Macdonald, General Secretary, National Bible Society of Scotland

The Revd Dr Robert McGhee, Minister, St Andrew's Church, Falkirk

The Revd Andrew T B McGowan, Minister, Causewayend Church, Aberdeen

The Revd Lewis R Misselbrook, formerly Adviser in Mission to Baptist Union of Scotland

The Revd Peter Neilson, National Organiser for Evangelism, Church of Scotland

The Revd Douglas A O Nicol, Minister, St Columba Church, Kilmacolm, Renfrewshire

The Revd Ray Sawers, Minister, Cranstoun, Crichton and Ford, with Fala and Soutra Churches, Midlothian

The Revd David C Searle, Minister of Hamilton Road Presbyterian Church, Bangor, Co. Down

The Revd Roger Simpson, Rector, St Paul's and St George's Episcopal Church, Edinburgh

The Revd Jock C Stein, Joint Warden, Carberry Tower (Church of Scotland Residential Centre), Musselburgh

The Revd William Still, Minister, Gilcomston South Church, Aberdeen

The Revd Lance B Stone, Minister, Hackney Group of Churches, United Reformed Church, London

Andy Thornton, Musician, formerly Youth Adviser, Presbytery of Glasgow

The Revd Chris Wigglesworth, General Secretary of the Department of World Mission and Unity, Church of Scotland

David F Wright, Senior Lecturer in Ecclesiastical History, New College, University of Edinburgh

The Revd David A Young, Minister, Kirkmuirhill Church, Lanarkshire

Introduction

The last few years have witnessed a rising level of interest in evangelism on the part of some at least of the Scottish Churches. The 'Presbytery Development Process' has become the focus of the Church of Scotland's national strategy for evangelism, which has led also to the appointment of national and regional organisers for evangelism. A major part of their work will lie in the promotion and co-ordination of evangelistic training and leadership at the regional or presbytery or congregational level. 'Scotreach' is the name of the three-year programme of preparation and activity to which the Baptist Union of Scotland has committed itself, and for which it has recruited the short-term services of a consultant in evangelism. A sharper awareness of the need for evangelism has been one outcome of the survey of Church attendance conducted by the National Bible Society of Scotland and Marc Europe, whose results were published in *Prospects for Scotland* (edited by P Brierley and F Macdonald, 1984). While for the most part not surprising, they challenged complacency and reinforced the growing conviction that evangelism must feature as high as anything on the Churches' agenda.

This book is offered as a contribution to the rediscovery of evangelism as a priority for every congregation in the Churches of Scotland. Evangelism may be defined briefly as the God-given task of presenting the good news of Jesus Christ in the power of the Holy Spirit in order that men and women and children may come to trust in God through him, accept him as their Saviour and serve him as their King in the fellowship of his Church in the world. It is concerned with communicating a specific message—a message that is not only about Jesus Christ but *is* Jesus Christ—with the aim of winning those who receive it to his allegiance. In whatever way it is carried out, evangelism involves making known the gospel of Christ—Christ clothed with the gospel—with a view to introducing people, through the work of the

Spirit, to the light and life of God that are found only in Christ.

This book's concentration on evangelism alone is not meant to imply that it is the sum and total of the mission of the Church, nor should its special focus on congregational evangelism be read as a judgment on evangelism in other contexts. But its production has been inspired by the conviction that what will count in the long run will be evangelism grounded in the local church. The congregation renewed for mission is God's primary evangelistic agency. Although one section of the book deals with evangelistic endeavour in a wider setting, at the level of the town or the presbytery, this too is approached in terms of co-operation between congregations. Where external resources or programmes are in view, the concern is with their contribution to the evangelistic commitment of the congregation itself.

How does the book set out to fulfil these aims? It is certainly not a manual of evangelism suitable for inclusion in a series of 'Know how to' or 'Teach yourself' handbooks. It does not invite readers to use it as an enquire-within-on-evangelism almanac. Nor, on the other hand, is it concerned to spell out at any length a theology of evangelism, important though this must be. In the main it is written out of the experience of those who have put their hands to the plough of congregational evangelism and have not turned back. The contributors bear testimony to what they believe God has called them to do in the orbit of the local church in the furtherance of its evangelistic task. Their aim is not to advertise 'successful' methods of evangelism, but to speak about patterns and approaches which they have followed and which, on the basis of this experience, they wish to commend to others. It is hoped that the range of contributions (which has necessitated briefer treatment than might otherwise have seemed desirable) will ensure a breadth of interest and appeal. The book reflects a number of variables: for example, in local community (from rural parish to inner city and city centre); in resources, both human (from teams of different kinds to one-person evangelism) and material; and in occasions (from special weeks to the routine meetings of Church organisations).

This focus on the congregation could be narrowed further—to the Sunday morning service. Since this is in most cases a congregation's sole meeting as 'church' during the week, what happens during that hour, or more largely, sets the tone for the whole life of the congregation. This is as true of evangelism as of any other dimension of the congregation's calling. If our worship is not informed by an evangelistic concern, it is doubtful whether the rest of our activity will be. Are our services of worship welcoming, open in spirit and ethos to the outsider, the visitor, the wider community? Or is the language of our worship that of an 'in-group', culturally separate, acceptable because of its comfortable familiarity to the faithful? So much depends in this area on the assumptions, great and small, that, so easily unquestioned, dictate what we do together Sunday by Sunday. We need to be more self-critical, not only about the 'message', more often implicit than explicit, that our worship conveys to the stranger and the uncommitted, but also about its impact on the congregation itself. Does it help to impart an evangelistic awareness to the regular attenders, sensitising them to their role in the congregation's evangelistic responsibility? Such questions carry no implication that .every service should be explicitly and directly evangelistic. They rather bid us ask ourselves how clearly the Church's worship articulates a sense of the unfinished task in which it is engaged, locally and to the ends of the earth.

Our hope is that this modest volume will be used by the Spirit of God to stimulate new initiatives in many a congregation, whether or not along any of the lines covered in its pages. (Far be it from our concern to *restrict* the ways in which the Churches fulfil their Lord's command to proclaim the gospel to every creature.) We suggest that it might form the basis of discussions on evangelism by Kirk Sessions, diaconates and vestries, as well as in Presbytery committees entrusted with promoting evangelistic endeavour in their area. In these and other ways it may serve as a further resource to prompt and provoke us to renewed faithfulness to our evangelistic calling.

The Missionary Parish

We have been seeking for a long time for a strategy of evangelism that might match the needs of the present day. Some of us within the Church of Scotland believe that we already have a tool in our hands which, reshaped, might well be the instrument we need.

The Church of Scotland is the national Church. This means primarily not a claim for special treatment or particular status, but an acceptance of the responsibility to provide 'the ordinances of religion' to every person resident in Scotland. It has sought to discharge this responsibility for the whole nation through the parish system. Every person resident in Scotland lives within a parish, which is the Christian responsibility of a congregation. Its minister has been inducted, not to the congregation only, but to the parish. In that parish system, re-examined, adapted, revitalised, we believe the key to a sound strategy of mission may well be found.

How the Parish System Operated

In the history of the Church of Scotland, the parish has served an almost exclusively pastoral role. It was accepted that Scotland was a Christian land. Its people were set within parishes to be cared for and, if necessary, disciplined, by the congregation to which they were attached. Children, as heirs of the covenant, were baptised into Christian fellowship, which was represented by the local congregation. Their nurture in the faith followed: in the home, in the school where work was very much overseen by the minister, and in the church. At the appropriate time, vows of full church membership were taken as young people came to years of understanding, and so the circle of pastoral care continued.

This represented an ideal which was, of course, never true to actual circumstances. There were always those who had separated themselves from the Church, and saw themselves as having no need of its pastoral care. But in many areas of pre-industrialised Scotland, the truth was near enough the ideal to be acceptable.

But industrialisation, with its large-scale uprooting and movement of population, played havoc with the notion of a national Church exercising country-wide pastoral care and nurture through the parish system. The Church did make efforts to modernise its parish structure. In various ways new parishes were created and new buildings erected, but these could never cope with the massive changes that had occurred. The cities had grown, new industrial towns had been created. In the welter of working class accommodation provided in the decades following the industrial changes, there was little sense among the new inhabitants of any relationship to a parish church.

And yet the old concept of the parish as a pastoral agency continued to be accepted. As long as people in sufficient numbers supported the parish church, the purely pastoral emphasis continued. Children were baptised, nurtured in the faith and brought to confirmation of their vows. It was possible to forget the others, to close the eyes to the increasing numbers who were at no point brought in to the circle of pastoral nurture and care.

Some of course did see the need, and from time to time attempts were made to meet it. Some heroic ministries were wrought out in the slum areas of our cities. Occasionally help from outside was sought, and special evangelistic efforts were made. But in the main, it has to be acknowledged that almost to our times, the parish system was seen solely as an instrument of pastoral nurture and care. As long as sufficient numbers enabled the life of congregations to continue, many went on using the parish system in its traditional way, despite the growing numbers who were becoming totally estranged from the Church and the Christian faith.

The Need for Change in the Parish System

If the parish system is to serve as the basic strategic model for a new effective outreach by the Church, if it is to be the instrument of a new evangelistic enterprise, then it must be reappraised, realigned, reshaped in a quite drastic way. It must be moved from serving a purely pastoral purpose, to the service of an evangelistic purpose; or, to combine these two vitally important concerns, the parish system must become the agent of an endeavour in pastoral evangelism.

It is to effect this change in thought and attitude and direction within our congregations that we must bend our best efforts.

Sector Ministries

To speak of the parish as the *area* of mission and the congregation as the *agent* of mission, is not to deny the need for specialist ministries in the great sectors of life. For life at home within the parish is not the only dimension to human existence in our times. Men and women go out to work. They pass through universities and colleges, they may have to spend time in hospitals or in prison. These settings are not merely areas in which time is spent, but represent major factors in making men and women what they are. We have realised the need for chaplains in industry, in hospitals, in universities, in prisons, to be with our people, to be involved in their situation, so that they may better understand and serve the mission of the Church in these sectors of life.

The Importance of a Reshaped Parish System

But the parish still retains its prime importance, and still represents, we would claim, the major instrument of evangelism in our time, if it can be reshaped for the purpose.

There is nothing new in this concept. It is a long time now since 'Tell Scotland', the great missionary movement, spoke of the congregation as the agent of mission in its own area, and spoke of mission as a continuous concern rather than an occasional activity. But congregations have been slow to learn and reluctant to change attitudes. As long as reasonable support was given to the local church, it continued to think of itself as a gathered fellowship, rather than as a missionary agency.

It has taken the growing realisation that we are losing ground continually, and at an alarming rate, to bring home to some at least an awareness that we cannot sit at ease in Zion. Through the falling away of recent decades, God has been speaking. It is not to preserve the Church that we must be missionary-minded, but because mission is part of the essential nature of the Church, part of our calling as Christians. Two major questions have to be answered if we are to work out a missionary strategy in terms of an adapted parish system. *First,* what do we mean by a developed missionary parish? And *second* (for we are speaking of the Church of Scotland with its Presbyterian system), how must the Presbytery encourage, assess and assist, if these missionary parishes are to be established within the bounds of Presbyteries throughout Scotland?

The Developed Missionary Parish

There is a very real sense in which the *first* question I have posed can only be fully answered by each congregation for itself. Minister, office-bearers and people must ask and seek an answer to the question: 'What does it mean for us in our own particular community to create a developed missionary parish?' The detailed answer can only be worked out in the context of each very differently set congregation.

But there are of course general guidelines, since similarities as well as differences exist. I quote now from the suggestions made in the report of the Mission Committee to the General Assembly of 1986. There should be:

> A significant group of Christian believers convinced of the truth of the gospel, inspired and assured in worship, sacraments, preaching, teaching and fellowship; praying regularly in community and in private for Christian work in the world; adequately equipped for ministry with leadership and office-bearers, committed to a priority for evangelism and the winning of new members; practising pastoral care for all its parish; encouraging and developing the gifts of all its members; funding these initiatives and supporting world mission as a natural response to the gospel; and engaged in active dialogue with other Churches and non-Christian groups.

In more summary form, we are seeking the formation throughout Scotland of congregations whose life and worship and fellowship are, in the best sense of the word, attractive, drawing those in the community around into their fellowship; congregations in which, under God, the clear preaching and teaching of the gospel will lead men and women to faith in Christ and will build them up in their faith; congregations who seek to know the real needs of their communities, and who, intelligently and compassionately, try to meet these needs in the name and spirit of Jesus.

These objectives of course will not be reached overnight or easily, but let congregations agree on these aims. Let them talk and pray together. Let them seek training and plan experiments in outreach. Let them be willing to accept assessment and guidance, and we shall begin to see movement.

The creation of developed missionary parishes, accepting the priorities of pastoral evangelism in their own communities, could well renew the whole Church.

Presbytery Oversight

The mention of assessment and guidance leads us to the *second* question we raised, concerning the part Presbytery has to play in the process.

The General Assembly of the Church of Scotland in 1985 placed the responsibility for evangelism throughout the land on the shoulders of Presbyteries, and in 1986 instructed them to review the role of their Home Mission Committees, so that they might effectively implement the Presbytery Development Process.

Presbyteries are encouraged to see their areas as units, sometimes representing very different needs and possibilities, but rich in gifts that may be used across parish boundaries. Sharing is to be encouraged at every possible level: in common prayer, in Presbyterial training conferences, in Festivals of Faith, and in the creation of missionary task forces.

An important task of encouragement by assessment and guidance can be fulfilled by Presbyteries acting not in any inquisitorial attitude, but in a spirit of encouragement, establishing personal contact with congregations, providing practical criteria for assessing each aspect of development, identifying areas that need encouragement, and helping to make known and available, resources in personnel and materials.

Some congregations within their own resources can work out and achieve the goal of a developed missionary parish. Other congregations need guidance and encouragement and help. It is for Presbyteries to take the overall view, to provide assistance as they can, and so to play their part in the renewal of the Church for mission.

Missionary Congregations

We have spoken of the developed missionary parish in terms of the Church of Scotland system. The title of this chapter—'The Missionary Parish'—makes that reference necessary. But any Christian fellowship, whatever its denominational attachment, is set within a community, and it is the Christian duty of every such congregation to see itself, not as a gathered fellowship serving the interests of its own members, but as an agent of mission developing its life and worship and service, so that it can more effectively minister in Christ's name to the needs of the people around.

Indeed it will often be found that pastoral and evangelistic work in particular communities can best be done as congregations of different denominations bring together their strengths and their gifts and their resources to serve their communities together. This kind of ecumenical effort, not dictated by structural schemes from above, but growing out of shared witness, will be a very positive strengthening of the missionary endeavour.

Negative and Positive Motivation

There are two final factors which ought to motivate God's people to work for the creation of the developed missionary parishes we have described: one factor we might describe as a present negative, and the other as a continuing positive.

The negative is the despairing need of our own times. Every recent survey has shown a falling number of committed church members, a decreasing knowledge of the Christian faith, and all this in an age which desperately needs the gospel.

The positive word has reference to the fact that missionary endeavour is not a harsh duty laid upon Christians, so that their major reaction may well be a sense of guilt, rather than an overflow of their own life in Christ. If our people can be encouraged to enter more fully and joyously into worship, to reclaim the fullness of the faith that is theirs, to deepen the fellowship of the Church and enlarge the circle of its care, then very freely and spontaneously will come the desire for missionary outreach, and so once again will the Church be the agent of God's mission in our land.

I
Evangelism in the Setting of the Congregation

1

Congregational Surveys:
Preparation for Evangelism

Evangelism is not the spring or autumn sale. It is the daily business of the shop. When we open the pages of the New Testament, four things are immediately evident:

(1) The Church at that time was a living demonstration of the presence of Jesus Christ in the community. It was—for all its faults—what it preached and it preached by what it was.

(2) Evangelism was both natural and primary. All organisation existed to facilitate its evangelistic role. Organisation did not exist to perpetuate itself. The sense of the guiding presence and power of the Holy Spirit was overwhelming.

(3) The witness of the Church flowed out through every member in everything they were and did and said. The greatest resource God has given to the Church is its members and their gifts. Today too little of it is used or expected to be used.

(4) Members were nurtured to know their faith, to apply it to every part of their daily lives and to share it with others.

To these things we are being recalled in our day. It is a matter of positive vision, of steady building and of a new call to obedience to Jesus and a discipleship filled with his Spirit. 'As the Father has sent me,' he says, 'even so I send you' (John 20:21, RSV).

One means of providing vision and direction is the congregational survey.

The Aim

The aim is to allow a team of three outsiders to look at the local church and the parish for one week, to attempt to see where the church is, to sum up the opportunities, the resources and the potential the church has and to suggest a strategy or some positive steps forward to further the witness of the church in those particular areas. The survey is always positive and encourages all it can. The three members of the survey team are carefully chosen. All need to be relaxed and loving people with insight and analytical ability. One should be a minister, one should know the local church fairly well and it is an advantage for one to be a woman. They work closely as a team.

The Method

The team live with the local church to be surveyed for about a week. They begin by spending one or two hours with the minister seeking to understand how he sees his church, its opportunities and potential and what visions of mission he has. A list of questions to ask him is given below.

The mornings are spent visiting representative church members by appointment. Each visit lasts about an hour. The afternoons are spent looking round the town, speaking to helpful people (council, district nurse, welfare, police, and so on), visiting some homes around the church building and talking to people in the street about the town and its churches and how they see them, and about their hopes, fears and longings about life and about God. This is best done on a one-to-one basis and can be moving or humorous. But it is always instructive. The evenings are spent visiting the various church organisations, meetings and house groups, getting the 'feel' of them and their purpose and effectiveness. This should include a meeting with the elders and listening to them discuss among themselves the church and its future possibilities.

The team should be given bed and breakfast for the week by church members and have other meals with as many members as possible. A great deal is learned by informal chatting over meals. (A questionnaire can also be used—see below.) The team will also need a quiet, comfortable room somewhere where they can meet, talk, think and pray together each day.

Following the Visit

The survey team go through all they have gathered, think and pray about it and try to pick out points where the church has possibilities and resources for advance. (See *Love Won Another* by Lewis and Molly Misselbrook, Marshall Pickering, 1987, for guidance on evangelism and church advance.) A report is written for the church in positive terms, then reconsidered and rewritten.

The skill of a good report is in assessing how far a church can move at one time. If a report suggests much more than a church can face then it is likely to be wholly rejected. It must praise, inspire, encourage and be seen to be possible.

The report is for the minister and elders of the local church. How much they pass on to members is left to them. They should have a couple of retreats or several special meetings to think and pray through the report and decide on action.

After six months it is helpful for the survey team to meet with the local minister and elders to talk over what has or has not been done.

General Questionnaire

Because it is impossible to meet and talk with all church members, a general questionnaire given out to everyone on one Sunday morning is useful. Careful preparation should lead the people to understand how helpful it will be to the survey team if they will complete it, that it is anonymous and totally confidential and that honesty (and no conferring) is all-important.

Here is the questionnaire we have used:

THIS QUESTIONNAIRE IS CONFIDENTIAL AND ANONYMOUS

Please do not sign it unless you wish to.

1 Are you a member   (   )

    just a regular attender   (   )

    a casual attender   (   ) (please tick)

2 Are you male   (   )

    female   (   ) (please tick)

3 Are you single   (   )

    married   (   )

    widowed   (   )

    other   (   ) (please tick)

4   Age (please tick)

15–20	20–25	25–35	35–45	45–55	55–65	65–75	75+

5   How far from the church building do you live? (miles)

$-\frac{1}{2}$	–1	1–2	2–3	3–4	4–5	5+

6   What made you join our church rather than any other?

7   Did you first come through

        your partner   (   )

        your family   (   )

        a friend   (   )

        other   (   ) (please tick)

        please specify: _____

8   For how long have you been attending our church?

–1 yr	1–2 yrs	2–3	3–5	5–10	10–20	20–30	30+

9   What do you feel are the greatest things about our church? What are its strong points?

10   What three things would you alter or add if you could to improve the life and effectiveness of this church for Jesus?

11   What is the most important thing in life for you personally? What do you live for?

12   Why do you go to church?

13   Write below the 4 most important things you think a church of Jesus exists for. If you think we are already doing well in any of these things put a tick in the box at the end:

Things a church exists for:	Doing well
1	
2	
3	
4	

14 Does this church help you to worship and serve the Lord Jesus

      in your work?   yes (   ) no (   )

      in your home?   yes (   ) no (   )

      in your relationships? yes (   ) no (   )

      in the community?   yes (   ) no (   ) (please tick)

15 What further help would you like the church to give you in your Christian life?

16 Any other comments you would like to make about the life, witness and possibilities of this church?

(*A collective summary of the forms is made and included in the report*)

Questions to ask the Minister

1 General description of town or parish.
2 Characteristics of its people.
3 Changes taking place.
4 Opportunities for presentation of the gospel present.
5 The hindrances to the gospel present.
6 General description of church and congregation.
7 Characteristics and spread of members.
8 The main aims of the last three years.
9 The main aims for the next three years.
10 What nurture and training are given to new converts?
11 How are gifts discovered, developed and deployed?
12 How are leadership gifts discovered and developed?
13 Whether there are house groups, their aim and effectiveness.
14 How the church is involved in the life of the community as light and salt (Matthew 5:13–16,AV).
15 What ways of witness or evangelism have been used in the last five years and how effective were they?

16   What are your visions, strategy and objectives to win this parish for Jesus Christ?
17   How pastoral care works in the church.
18   What the church is doing about problems of unemployment, race *etc*, in the church and in the community.
19   What points would you have to put in a report on this church if you were a member of the survey team?
20   How do you see your role as minister of this church and servant of the purposes of Jesus here and now?
21   Relationships with other churches in the neighbourhood and the wisdom of working together in mission.

Church Organisations

Making comments on church organisations is difficult. Comparisons are invidious and some leaders find their significance (or even their identity) in their organisation.

For this reason we do not comment in our reports but ask the leaders of each organisation to meet in their own group to think and pray through the following questions before God:

1   What are our aims?
2   Are these primary aims in the New Testament?
3   Are we achieving those aims?
4   Would there be some more simple or direct way of achieving them?
5   Are our aims and work an integral part of church work and aims?
6   Are you keeping fresh and effective as Christian leaders with training and refresher courses?
7   If you are dealing with children, are you including their parents in the pastoral charge given to you by Jesus?
8   Are you now and always willing to lay yourselves, your work and your organisation at the feet of Jesus subject to his Lordship and totally at his disposal either to cease or to continue as he wills?

The Spread of Members

The local church is asked to provide a large map of the parish with coloured pins to mark the residences of communicant members and attenders. A glance at where the pins are thick and where thin can be revealing.

The Graph

The church is also asked to provide a graph of membership figures for the last 20 years with notes of ministries, outreach efforts and changes of population during that time. This can help us see what methods have or have not been effective in this parish.

New Converts

Converts of the last five years should be asked:

1 What was it that prompted you to be interested in becoming a Christian?
2 Were you influenced by a friend, a sermon, a book, your family or anything else (please say what)?
3 What made you come to this church and not to another?
4 Have you found it easy or difficult to become integrated into the fellowship here?

These questions pinpoint strong points on which the church should concentrate, as well as weak points to be looked at.

The Gifts Card

At the same time as the congregational questionnaire is being given out, a card can be given to discover the gifts and talents of members.

Full information on this is in a pamphlet by Hugh Wyllie entitled *Labourers Wanted for the Vineyard: How to Identify and Use Our Members' Gifts*, published by the Stewardship Committee of the Church of Scotland. In his scheme, members are visited by picked people and invited to set down on a card provided their gifts, talents, interests, hobbies and work. The understanding is that the church can approach them again if a need arises for the help of someone with their particular gifts or skills. This could be adapted so that the picked people called in person to collect both the card and questionnaire and to give any help needed in understanding the form or card or their purpose.

A register of gifts and skills is then compiled by the church and a small group thinks and prays through it to see how the work and purposes of Jesus might be advanced by calling the gifts and skills into use. Some 6–10 per cent of the membership generally have gifts for evangelism and very many others have supporting gifts.

Thus the outreach and progress suggested by the survey team is complemented by the list of resources in the membership.

Conclusion

A survey can be of great help to the thinking, planning and vision of the local church. But the most important point is that the church should be united in love and purpose, wide open to the Spirit of Jesus in prayer and with the outward look of openness to others in love.

The little body of men and women meeting in the upper room in Jerusalem could not just settle down to singing hymns, listening to sermons and organising and going to meetings. Had they done this the Church would have been extinct in half a century. Instead the gospel spread like a living flame all over the known world. It could not be kept in. Please God, it will overflow like that again in our time.

2

House Groups and Church Organisations

'Do come along to our church!' This is a common enough remark, but what do we want people to find in 'our church'? Is our expectation that our first point of contact with those lacking Christian faith and commitment will be on their arrival at one of our church services? It may be, and God may bring them to know himself on the very first experience they have of worshipping with the people of God. But to write about the powerful evangelistic impact of the vibrant worship of a congregation is not my remit. Starting from our experience in Holy Trinity Church, Wester Hailes, Edinburgh, I want to look at the way various organisations in a church can be a means of reaching those who are not believers.

House Groups

More and more congregations are introducing these in some form into the regular structures of the life of the congregation. Their primary purpose is one of upbuilding and encouraging members of the church through worship, study and fellowship in much smaller units. But can they incorporate an evangelistic function as well?

Our experience in Holy Trinity Church indicates that house groups can be an effective means of outreach to those who are not Christians. From the first introduction of house groups in our congregational life, their evangelistic potential was realised. The principle of establishing them *only* within the parish of Wester Hailes was a key factor in this. We wanted them to be 'lighthouses' in the various parts of our vast, very needy parish. It would have been easy to develop additional house groups in the surrounding housing areas, but one of the results might have been the encouragement of 'a cosy fellowship' mentality.

The choice of homes as meeting places for the house groups requires careful consideration. We have always had many offers of homes, sometimes even from people who are very much on the fringe of the congregation. The host and hostess of a group are also key people in terms of its evangelistic impact when it becomes known that a part of the church meets in their home. Hosts and hostesses need to be those who commend the Lord Jesus to others by their day to day living and are well thought of by their neighbours. Very practical factors need to be borne in mind as well: Is the house easily accessible for the elderly or less able physically? Will it be big enough to hold a group of up to 15 or more? Will the neighbours object if there is singing, or a lot of coming and going in the stair? Are there young children in the family who may be a distraction if they are up and about during the meeting?

On the whole our experience has indicated that it is easier to appoint leaders who are not the host and hostess, so that the latter can be left free to attend to welcoming, organising tea, and so on. In training house group leaders, one of the subjects dealt with is the way they welcome the new person. Some leaders have found this quite daunting, especially if the visitor is argumentative or reluctant to accept the approach of the group to the Bible as God's Word, or the pattern of the evening's activity. In such instances the leaders have to be ready to operate with a good deal of flexibility, so that a prepared approach can be changed or adapted at very short notice if a new person arrives who seems to have little or no Christian understanding. That makes for exciting and challenging leading—and even more reliance on God the Holy Spirit.

Nothing could be more off-putting to a newcomer to a house group than to be expected to know his or her way about the Bible, to be asked to read aloud, or even to take part in any way. Some of the topics shared for prayer together may also have to be tailored in the light of visitors, although on the whole our groups have carried on their practice of having open prayer even when non-Christians are present, as we should not underestimate the powerful impact that it may have on them.

In Holy Trinity Church we have found over the years that the house group study materials already available are rarely suitable for our needs, and we have had to produce our own. This has the great advantage that they can be prepared with non-Christians as well as Christians in mind, and often a question may be set which gives the leader the opportunity to draw the group naturally on to the message of the gospel, or to the sharing of personal experience of conversion and new life in Jesus. Even when the material has not obviously lent itself to an evangelistic Bible study, our experience has been that time and time again the Holy Spirit makes God's Word relevant to everyone in the group.

It is a very real help, occasionally, for a special 'open night' to be arranged by the group. Our first experience of these was in the home of a senior citizen who made marvellous contacts with her neighbours and others at the bus stop. The pattern was usually to have a speaker who shared his or her testimony and then chatted with people over tea. These meetings were frequently held in afternoons to enable elderly people to attend more easily. Since that first experiment, all the other house groups have developed this idea, particularly at Christmas time. One group even held a summer mini-bus outing to the country. In today's world, Christian videos are a natural medium to use, and there is an increasing range of suitable material for this kind of outreach by a house group.

Another house group has a weekly children's Bible Club as an offshoot. Leading up to Christmas the children prepare a special 'event' (singing, drama) to present to the 'open night' to which parents are especially invited. An amazing number of adults and children cram into that home to see it. Some of the parents and children have had no other contact with church activities as yet.

Evangelistic visitation is being tackled by some house groups, especially where the elders and pastoral assistants for the district are also in the house group within the district. It is hoped that the pastoral teams will use the house group membership increasingly in systematic visitation and also in making contact with newly reoccupied houses and with those who have expressed some interest in the gospel or the church.

Church Organisations

Like most other congregations, we in Holy Trinity have a number of organisations according to age and sex, as well as others which are open to all and may be less usual in a church.

Nowadays we do not find large numbers of children flocking to Sunday School. Most of the children around the church on a Sunday are in the families of church members. With our emphasis on the children as part of God's worshipping people, all except the very youngest participate in the monthly Celebration service, and on other Sundays, children aged three to eight years go out to Beginners and Primary Sunday School after about a third of the morning service. The children aged eight years and upwards share in the whole morning service and remain behind afterwards for Junior Workshop, which aims to apply the teaching from that morning service to their needs.

In these ways we seek to root our 'church children' firmly into the family of the church and in particular its worship. In the light of that, we expect our main organised outreach to youngsters to take place during the week, in line with Roy Joslin's observation in his book *Urban Harvest* (Evangelical Press, 1982) that the 'best time for some Sunday Schools is a weeknight evening' (p 138).

Uniformed organisations have not been a strong feature of our young people's work in recent years. Instead new clubs have been developed to integrate the children's work very clearly into the structure of the church's life. Mention has already been made of the midweek children's Bible Club held by house group members in a home, and there have been three other similar groups also held in homes. Once children overcome any initial shyness about being in someone's home, they quickly adapt and even tend to behave better than when on church premises. However the lack of space does limit what can be attempted in terms of games and activities.

The past few years have seen the encouraging development of the Friday evening Adventurers Boys Club (ABC for short) for boys aged eight to eleven. Many who attend are not church members' children, but they are drawn into the life of the church through the Club, by being reminded regularly of the monthly Celebration services and Junior Workshop. More recently a Monday night Adventurers Girls Club has been started with the same aim of introducing girls in the same age range to the Lord Jesus. As with the boys' work, the striking feature of this group is the keen interest which is taken in the Christian teaching focus by children who otherwise have no Christian background or encouragement.

Because children are being reached from right outside the ambit of Christian influence, nothing can be presumed about their grasp of basic Bible teaching, although all would hear at least something at the assemblies held in the local Primary Schools. This means that again much of the material available for use with children has to be adapted quite considerably. It is often quicker and easier for the leaders in these children's Clubs to prepare their own, using vocabulary and concepts which will be meaningful to the children. It does not really help to reiterate ideas of two-parent families living in pleasant semi-detached houses with gardens when so many are in single-parent families living in stairs or in high-rise blocks!

Teenage work can be a very great challenge, and earlier experiments with a Youth Club on our church premises were both costly and discouraging and had to be discontinued. Recently it has been a joy to see the growth of very lively work amongst the 12-15 year olds (boys and girls mixed) in a group called the Power and Light Company (PLC for short). This takes the place of the traditional Bible Class and meets on a Friday evening. It also has the scope to go on outings, have weekends away, hold all-night hikes, and much more. This approach is clearly one which appeals to a number of teenagers in our kind of parish (and some from outside it too) and the leaders have been able to draw quite a number of the members of the PLC into the worship life of the congregation, for example by inviting them to take part in the services. The next step is to persuade the 15 year olds to go on to the Youth Fellowship held after the Sunday evening service. Again encouragingly this has become a thriving group after a quiescent period.

Single-sex adult organisations are still a feature of most congregations and ours is no exception. Far from merely attracting church members, the Woman's Guild and Young Woman's Group now consistently draw in those who have no live church connection or clear Christian commitment. Programmes have to be planned bearing that in mind, and informal 'friendship' evangelism is vital. In the past a women's Keep Fit Group (with a crèche) was also held one morning a week, and this attracted a number of young mothers, some of whom subsequently found their way into the church Café and the Way-in Group (see below) and into real faith and church membership.

Never having attended one of the regular men's meetings, I have to write about them from a distance. After a tentative beginning with a Men's Fellowship, specifically evangelistic evenings were developed, using the Lounge Suite of the local hotel, rather than the church premises, in order to help those right outside the church to feel more at ease. The practice has been to invite a speaker who will share his testimony, perhaps with the backing of some music led by our music group. The level of attention among the men who have been attracted has been quite remarkable. They seem to feel very much at home in this type of gathering, where there is plenty of time to talk over supper after the speaker has finished. This can seem like slow work, but it has helped to give a definite focus to the evangelistic work among men.

A feature of the church's outreach for the past ten years has been a thrice weekly Church Café (one afternoon and two mornings). Here the emphasis is on friendship and acceptance and we have never had an evangelistic 'spot' as in the Christian Coffee Club approach. The key lies in Christians being available to help at the Café and to be prepared prayerfully to speak to people informally—'gossiping the gospel'— whenever an opportunity arises. This too is long-term work but we have been encouraged to see some fruit from it in several regular Café attenders eventually becoming Christians and taking (for them) the big step of attending church services, house groups and new members' classes. The Café has always been a place where unemployed people could come, but quite recently a special 'drop-in' club for the unemployed, called The Gate, has started, largely attracting men so far. There is clearly real potential in this for drawing in those who have little or no Christian contact.

For almost as long as the Church Café has functioned another group has met fortnightly on a Thursday morning for basic Bible Study, calling itself the Way-in Group. This has been directed at the person who feels very unfamiliar with the Bible. No prior knowledge is ever presumed; some might have difficulty in finding Matthew's Gospel if handed a Bible for the first time. The approach is simple, with questions to bring out the meaning of the passage, usually from one of the Gospels as we systematically work through it, although parts of Acts and Romans have been covered too. The participants in the Way-in Group change as people come to faith, grow in understanding and move on to attend house groups and the church's midweek fellowship for Bible study and prayer, but for some it has indeed been the *way in* to the kingdom of God.

I have described a variety of approaches which are possible in one parish, but may not all be relevant in other congregational situations. Our concern is that they express the life of a fellowship wanting to be open to the Holy Spirit and to be renewed by him to bear witness to the Lord Jesus Christ. Although the focus of this chapter is the place of house groups and church organisations in the evangelistic outreach of a congregation, it would be unbalanced to conclude from it that we *rely* on such organisations in our evangelism. It is our conviction that individual Christians and Christian families witnessing to friends and neighbours with the attractiveness of the love of Jesus is the greatest evangelistic method of all.

3

Baptisms, Marriages and Funerals

Baptisms

It must be clear to everyone that there are difficulties and tensions in maintaining dignity and discipline in the administration of baptism. The minister's problem is three-fold: *first*, to be faithful to the teaching of the Bible; *second*, to communicate something of that teaching to those bringing their children for baptism; and *third*, to welcome and win for Christ those who come. It is all too easy, in trying to achieve the first two of these aims, to fail dismally in the third. How often, instead of families being won for Christ, they have been turned away, even embittered. And the minister is left with a hollow satisfaction that he has been 'faithful'.

Those who come looking for baptism will fall, broadly speaking, into three categories: (a) those who are regular attenders, members who are fairly close to the heart of the fellowship—it is always a joy to have such couples coming to ask for their child to be baptised; (b) others who are members of our congregation but who only occasionally attend church, and appear to have little or no idea of what real Christian commitment is; and (c) there are those who have no real church connection at all, but who feel that they are somehow depriving the child unless it is baptised—probably Granny has insisted that they 'hae the bairn done'. It is the last two categories we must think about, for our purpose is not only to preserve order and discipline in the church, but also to win men and women for Christ. And there is no doubt that the occasion of a child's baptism can be a crucial evangelistic opportunity.

The Nominal Member

From a strictly legal point of view (at least within the Church of Scotland), where one or other of the parents is a communicant member of the church, the couple have the right to claim baptism for their children, and the minister ought not to refuse. But that is no excuse for allowing the ceremony to be a formality.

I am sure that the first few minutes of the minister's meeting with a couple are quite critical. He is going to convey an impression which will be stamped indelibly on that couple's heart and mind. His attitude must be one of friendship, welcome and reassurance. He is there to love, to pastor, to win. This may well be his first and last great opportunity with this family. A suspicious, guarded, reserved attitude will immediately distance the couple from him and create a barrier. Once that barrier is there, it is hard to build a bridge across it. The friendly, welcoming approach is by no means inconsistent with careful and faithful explanation of all that is involved in baptism. Nor does it prevent the minister from being faithful to his understanding of a covenant theology of baptism. On the other hand, failure in this first contact can set a couple back for years, robbing them of a significant period of involvement in a Christian fellowship. I have seen this happen on more than one occasion.

The Non-Member

Again, those first few minutes of contact are so important. We are there to bring people in, not to keep them out. We are in a position of strength, and the young couple are in a position of weakness. It would be all too easy to be clever and smart with them, to ask questions and make statements which leave them struggling, out of their depth, and to which they cannot possibly reply. So what we say must be on a level that is realistic and can be easily understood.

My own practice for many years now has been to seek to be positive: 'Yes, I would love to baptise your baby . . . *but* baptism, by the law of the Church, is for children of communicant members'. I then suggest that they begin attending straight away, suggesting that I will arrange to see them again when they have been coming consistently for five or six weeks.

I am only too well aware of the danger of bringing people to the Lord's Table for the wrong reasons. And I have never insisted on full-communicant membership of the parent(s) before I baptise. But I have seen, on many occasions, couples won to Christ because they were invited to church by a minister whom they felt had welcomed them and befriended them. Some are simply not interested enough to come. But some are. We thank God for those who do come, and come again and again.

So often, church has been rejected as boring and irrelevant through bad Sunday School experiences in childhood. I am sure that tens of thousands in Scotland today refuse to attend church because of disastrous memories indelibly imprinted in their sub-conscious. But now that they are older, able to think conceptually, and have before them the awesome responsibility of bringing up a family in a pagan society, they are ready to listen with open ears. To attend a service where God is manifestly present, and where the Word is preached simply, clearly, and with power, produces in them a remarkable and positive response which can grow into living faith in Christ.

The Baptismal Class

There are two approaches to instruction. One emphasises the need to be converted for those who bring their children. I suppose that this is a valid method. But the approach I have always taken, which has been so often fruitful, is to concentrate on the Christian upbringing of children. Having explained as simply as I can the difference between the visible and invisible Church (using the parable of the Tares and the Wheat), I ask the question of how one moves from being only a professing Christian to being a 'born again Christian'. And I seek to answer this by showing that God will make use of their presence within the fellowship, their own Christian nurture of their child, and their faithfulness to the baptismal vows, to achieve this. We have made a practice of following up our interest in the children about four years after baptism with complimentary copies of *Simon and Sarah* booklets (published by Scripture Union), and it has been the parents' use of these with their children, together with faithful attendance at church, which has reaped the harvest for Christ.

Marriages

I have to confess that I have never found in weddings an immediate occasion for the presentation of the gospel. I cannot accept the view held by some that Christian marriage is only for believers. It has always appeared to me that marriage is a divine ordinance, and is for all mankind, whatever their creed. And part of the witness of the Church is to administer Christian marriage. The Lord's Day, one day of rest in seven, might offer an analogy. For the Lord's Day is the loving gift of God to all, for their rest and restoration, whether they are believers or not. And it has been the rejection of that gift that has brought so many into the doctors' surgeries demanding sedatives; it is the rejection of that gift which is responsible in part for the break-up of so many families, who no longer spend a quiet day together. Similarly, in marriage God has given a whole way of life to mankind, with the promise of security and happiness when that way of life is followed.

There is neither time nor space in this chapter to think about the problem of divorcees seeking Christian marriage. Studies have already been published on this thorny problem. Nor is there space to consider the problems of counselling the bride who is already pregnant; or to discuss how a minister deals with a girl who professes to be a Christian but who wants to marry an avowed non-Christian.

Suffice to say that weddings undoubtedly offer the minister a foundation on which to build relationships for the future. It is in preparing for the wedding that I first introduce the subject of baptism of any future children the couple may have. I also urge the couple to attend church regularly before their wedding. While I do not think one can legitimately insist on church attendance, I have found that a minority of those I have married, and who have come to church at my request before the ceremony, have stayed with us. But I would have to admit that it has been in later contact, when children arrived, that real progress has been made in bringing them to Christ.

To sum up, the parish minister must see marriages in the wider context of his whole relationship with the people of his parish. Contacts are made with families, guests, relatives, as well as with the bride and groom, which count significantly in the way a community sees their minister. Is he approachable? Is he genuine? Does he care about people? Is he a man one could turn to in the hour of need? The minister is on public view at a wedding more than anywhere else. And in the most unexpected and apparently insignificant ways, he is placarding himself to a whole parish. I have often felt that had I been a holier man, these occasions would have offered opportunities (of which I might still have been unaware) of presenting the challenge of Jesus Christ to people I would never normally meet.

Funerals

As with all one's daily contacts as a minister, those with whom we deal in bereavement situations fall into three broad categories: (a) the dear friends who have supported their minister for many years, and whose passing is both sorrow and joy—sorrow to lose them and joy that they are with Christ; (b) the ones we have come to know just a little, but with whom we have not been able to form a close relationship; and (c) those whom we have never met, but whom we are asked to bury because they are parishioners.

It hardly needs to be said that funerals are bound to offer the minister very great opportunities to present Christ to men and women. And yet, so many ministers will say that it is one of the hardest tasks of all to use that opportunity for real, effective evangelism. I would offer a few principles which I believe should guide those of us called to conduct funeral services.

First, we must be meticulous in our attentiveness to pastoral care. What I mean is that it is really unforgivable—however harassed we may be—either to fail to visit as soon as possible after we have heard of a death, or to fail to revisit after the funeral service. That basic courtesy on our part is surely a minimum we must offer.

Second, we must care enough to give of ourselves, both in our visits in the home, and in our conduct of the service. So often I have returned home from a funeral and my wife, sensing at once my exhaustion, has asked, 'Do you *have* to give so much of yourself for people you've never even met?' The answer must be that Christ gave of himself to all who came to him.

Third, we must listen. On occasion, impatient relatives will try to silence the broken-hearted widow as she pours out her story of grief. But the minister who is seeking to love for Christ's sake will take time and be quiet so that he can hear the full account. For even as he listens, the grieving one senses whether or not he really cares.

Fourth, we must not offer false hope or confidence. To share in someone's grief is not the same as offering future hope. And if a man has lived and died godlessly, and a distraught widow is clutching at straws to console herself that he is now 'at rest', we do the gospel no service to assure her that he is. I have never found my offering sympathy and comfort to the living to be incompatible with simply saying of the departed that God is utterly just and righteous, and will reward everyone according to his ways.

Fifth, in our conduct of the funeral service, we have the greatest opportunity to present Christ. There is the reading of Scripture. I know of at least one person who was converted as I read the Word of God. We should pour all that we have into making the Word beautiful, glorious, simple, Christ-centred—the very Word of God to those listening. As I come to the Scripture reading, whether the service is in some humble home, in some gloomy backstreet funeral parlour, or in one of those specially-designed-for-sorrow crematoria, I always brace myself, and silently call on the Holy Spirit's power as I open the Scriptures and begin to read the precious Word of Life! After the reading, comes the prayer. I know that praying is not, and should not be, preaching. But surely in our prayer, as well as bearing up those who are grieving, and giving thanks for the life and love of the deceased, we must offer thanks to God for the hope we have in Christ. And it is then that the radiance of the Lord can shine forth. Our blessing God for salvation in prayer should, I feel, be in pictorial language, rather than full of theological jargon which will lose and baffle the bereaved. The birth, life, death and resurrection of Christ can all be spoken of in prayer in the simplest of terms, using word pictures, rather than concepts such as incarnation, vicarious suffering, atonement, justification, and so on. Our Lord himself is our authority for this, for he is the one who says, 'Come to me, all of you who are tired from carrying heavy loads' (Matthew 11:28,GNB) and 'Behold, I stand at the door, and knock: if any man hear my voice, and open the door, I will come in tò him, and will sup with him, and he with me' (Revelation 3:20, AV). Christ's words, more than anyone else's in Scripture, teach us to communicate eternal truths pictorially.

Sixth and finally, very often the great opportunity arises in the post-funeral contacts, as the grieving relative is waiting with deep questions which have been raised through all that has been experienced over the past few weeks. (I say 'weeks' because I deliberately wait for a week or two before I pay the post-funeral visit. I have found that it is better to wait until a measure of composure has been regained, and the stream of visiting relatives and friends has dried up, before returning.) What guidance can possibly be given, other than to say that we must always be ready to recognise the opportunities the Holy Spirit gives us, and to take them sensitively and lovingly?

I have seen many coming into fellowship with the body of Christ through the death of a loved one. But it has generally been through the overall contact that I have had with them, rather than through some particular conversation, or spoken word. Once again, as with baptisms and weddings, the almost indispensable background of all our work is a Christian fellowship where the awareness of God's presence is immediate, where the Word is clearly preached in relevant, living terms, and where the warmth of the welcome cannot but be recognised by those who come to worship. I know only too well the dilemma such a statement creates. What of the newly arrived minister who finds his congregation cold and lifeless? What platform has he got on which to base the work of evangelism? The only answer is that the work of creating a living, caring fellowship belongs to the Holy Spirit whose work of creation always begins with nothing (by definition). It is the same work as bringing to living faith those whose children we baptise, whose bereaved we bury, and whose marriages we conduct. The fact that he delights to use the living, caring, worshipping fellowship will not hinder him in the early days when no such fellowship appears to us to exist. The marvel is that he uses us at all. But he does, and as we co-operate with him, dealing kindly and gently, yet faithfully and honestly, with those who come to us, his silent work is done, and the harvest is reaped by those who have sown in tears, and who are by nothing discouraged.

4

Worship and Evangelism

In 1983 the Evangelism Committee of the Church of Scotland considered producing a book rather like the present one. Interestingly, however, no chapter was proposed on 'Worship and Evangelism'. For this there are reasons ancient and modern.

Christian tradition in the West was formed during the long period of Christendom, when church and society were symbiotic and enclosed. Mission, when it happened at all, was the work of fringe enthusiasts. The Reformation changed some things but not this. Calvin, for example, was in some ways an ecumenical figure, sharing in a network of Church leadership ranging from Scotland to Poland, but this was not mission (or ecumenism) in the New Testament or the modern sense. The Catholic missions in China and Japan ran into problems with Rome when they tried to relate worship to local culture. And the great Scottish missionary David Clement Scott, in what is now Malawi, seeking to build a 'Christianity which knew neither the division between Protestant and Catholic, nor even between East and West', received the dusty order from Edinburgh that he was there to build a church on sound Presbyterian principles and he had better not forget it!

In recent times, the advent of Crusade evangelism, and the reaction to it, tended to keep worship and evangelism apart. Evangelism was seen as something for one wing of the Church, and therefore to be tolerated, but no more. Yet the discerning would point out that even Crusade evangelism has a context of prayer and hymn-singing; and that a cross-section of people, asked how they came to active faith, would be most likely to include their experience of worship as an important factor—praise, prayer, preaching, even the blessing. They would also remind us that Communion is in the Scottish tradition a 'converting ordinance'. We do well, therefore, to examine more closely the relation of evangelism to worship, and the questions raised by new forms of both.

Augustine said, 'We baptise children in order that they may be converted'. How does conversion happen? Is it a gradual process best described by 'nurture', or a sudden step best described as 'commitment'? Whatever answer we give, evangelism is sure to happen in worship when God is present! You cannot draw near to God and be untouched. Evangelism may be defined in human terms, but its power lies in the work of the Holy Spirit.

A good starting point for understanding how the Spirit works is the life and worship of Israel. God revealed himself to Abraham and to his descendants, and called Israel to worship him. Christian worship is still the worship of Israel. We too are chosen by God to worship him. In the words of the Westminster Shorter·Catechism, to glorify God and to enjoy him for ever is 'man's chief end'.

The first four Commandments tell us: (a) worship must be of God alone; (b) worship must be in the right way (no images; only men and women represent God's image); (c) worship must be honest (in the words of Jesus, 'In spirit and in truth'); and (d) worship must be regular, visible and shared (implied by the Sabbath principle).

Worship in the Old Testament was clearly for the people of God. Foreigners had to be circumcised before they could share fully in the life and worship of Israel. This understanding is reflected in the Christian Church by the custom that enquirers must be baptised before they share in Communion.

However, another understanding began to grow within Israel, perhaps most obviously in the Book of Isaiah. Israel was called out not for its own sake, but for the sake of all nations, and called to be the light of the world. This destiny would be fulfilled when the Messiah came. Jesus says both, '*I* am the light of the world', of himself, and '*You* are the light of the world', of his disciples.

In Jesus, worship and mission, and therefore evangelism as a key part of mission, come together. Jesus is the Son of God who offers true worship to the Father; and Jesus is the one sent by God into the world, to Jew and to Gentile. If our worship is in the name of Christ, it means that we look to him as our leader. If our evangelism is in the name of Christ, it means that we look to him as our leader in that also.

Temple and House

But who exactly is Jesus? Christians have struggled to maintain with equal conviction that he is God, and that he is man. As man, his own worship and prayer was not a stained-glass window experience; he prayed with loud cries and tears. As a God-fearing Jew he joined in the worship of the synagogue, but he also disturbed the synagogue by claiming that God was bringing to life the words they treasured. Likewise the first disciples joined in Jewish Temple worship; but as their conviction grew that Jesus had fulfilled that whole tradition by his obedience in life and in death, so they were able to continue with worship and evangelism in home and hall when they were driven out of Jerusalem.

We find a two-fold pattern here. There is, *first*, the tradition of 'Temple worship' or indeed 'Synagogue worship', of public worship shaped over the centuries, led by carefully trained and authorised leaders. Since worship was, after all, for God, it was more important for people to learn to appreciate its riches than to change it to suit their culture or needs. (To quote Archbishop Runcie: 'Liturgy should be above people's heads, not beneath their feet'.) This tradition stressed the uniformity of worship, whether in the use of Latin in the old Roman mass, the Anglican Prayer Book, or indeed the 'high' and 'low' traditions of the Church of Scotland.

Then there is the *second* aspect of worship in homes and meeting places, less formal, more expressive, rooted in a local culture. In these contexts revival movements are less threatening to the 'Establishment', whether this refers to Scottish eighteenth-century kitchen meetings, for example, or contemporary charismatic house groups.

Together these two patterns make an attractive model for conservatives of every theological type—an ordered tradition of public worship, and opportunity for less formal worship in homes or the church hall. No doubt it corresponds to the Jewish tradition of weekly synagogue worship, and daily prayer in homes.

However that model is coming apart at the seams today, as Christian people are asking for that kind of 'overspill' on Sunday morning. In more biblical language, the old skins are failing to contain the new wine. Just as the worship of the first Christians outgrew the Temple tradition, which not only failed to contain the new worship but eventually expelled it, so public worship traditions today are finding it harder to cope adequately with the expectations and experience of Christian worshippers. Perhaps it is also a little like marriage: people today expect more of it, and at the same time it is easier to withdraw from it; and just as marriage needs to be well rooted in God's teaching about it to maintain its stability and fruitfulness, so worship needs to be rooted in revelation and only fertilised by our experience.

It is fashionable to see this in charismatic terms: one group sees the new wine stuff as spiritual and biblical, and rejoices in the exercise of gifts like tongues, prophecy and healing, with choruses and a bit of dance thrown in; another group condemns it all as of the flesh and definitely unbiblical. The first group quotes Scripture and speaks about miraculous healings; the second group quotes Scripture and speaks about the casualties.

The same kind of tension between the traditional and the new occurs when people want to change the language and imagery of hymns, and introduce popular music into worship. And here there is a definite relation to evangelism, whether for those inside or outwith the church.

Worship and Rapid Cultural Change

The need to relate to the contemporary world has not always been recognised by worship leaders. Although Calvin encouraged the French poet Marot to write metrical psalms, when Mission halls sprang up in the last century their Moody and Sankey hymns did not find favour in most churches. There was no recognition that the main worship tradition, whether liturgical or non-liturgical, itself might have to change radically.

Today the rate at which culture has changed has meant that our own children, let alone the millions outside the church, are strangers to our worship tradition. There is a sense, of course, in which worship will always be alien to self-centred humans of any age. Worship takes time and practice to grow on us. It was in this way that the King James Version of the Bible shaped the English language, and church music once shaped the culture of Europe. But for good or ill, since the 1960s the gap between church and culture has widened rapidly.

To test this, put the question: if three million out of the four million Scots who seldom attend worship were to be soundly converted, how many of them would happily start to attend traditional Presbyterian or Baptist or Catholic churches? Put the question another way round: are there more than a handful of people presently outside the life of the church who are starting to attend traditional churches, and then being brought to active faith?

This is of course a spiritual question. God is able to, and does use the most traditional church and pattern of ministry to reach people. But when surveys of church attendance find significant growth in the 'new' churches, and significant decline in the 'old' churches, and when experience with young people indicates that many are willing to take Jesus Christ seriously, but very few take the church seriously, it is time to ask whether the traditional models are working properly, or even whether they are the right models.

Scripture teaches that we are all by nature alienated from God. For some, that is a living memory; for others, who cannot remember a time when they did not love God, it is a humbling reminder that we worship only at God's invitation and by his enabling. If this is so, and if the Son of God became an alien to bring us back to God and one another, then we dare not allow barriers of culture to distance our fellow humans from the gospel and the life of worship to which all men and women are called. Worship should not change simply in order to be relevant, but in order that we will be more able to take others by the hand and lead them to Jesus, who will lead them and us to the Father. And because we too are children of our own age, such change, painful as it may be, will help us also to worship in spirit and in truth.

Our worship tradition is full of rich customs which can point us, insiders and outsiders alike, to Christ. The custom of bringing the Bible into the pulpit before the minister needs to be explained every so often, and related to the increasing use of pew Bibles. The meaning of great hymns can be brought out in a variety of ways—solo verses, reading over together (the way to get round an impossible tune with no alternative), testimony, meditation—although it is the Spirit himself who awakens our hearts to the real meaning of words of faith.

The old stained-glass tradition is now paralleled by a revival of banner-making, along with church art which is biblical and theological, not sentimental. The sacrament of baptism is profoundly evangelical; and while it is right to baptise 'in the face of the congregation', it may be appropriate sometimes to take the congregation out of the building. Two young men were baptised in the harbour of a Dundee parish in 1986.

There are however two areas where change in worship practice could help evangelism and integrate the two more fully.

Leadership of Worship: Minister and People

In Scotland the Old Testament pattern of the priest leading worship for Israel has prevailed. This was understandable in the days when nearly all Scots were baptised and the church was full of people carefully nurtured in home and Sunday School—if those golden days really existed! But today congregations are composed of a range of people, from insiders to outsiders (describe them how you will). The gospel needs to be explained simply, not taken for granted. Opportunities for response should be given, varying from a vestry open for counselling after worship, to a full-blown 'appeal'. An increasingly common practice is for a group of recognised leaders to continue with a quiet ministry of prayer and counselling at the front of the church while the congregation as a whole chat, drink tea or leave the church. Such opportunity can be taken in a very natural way, sometimes accompanied by quiet music or simply the buzz of conversation in another part of the church which gives ample privacy.

Although attitudes to ordained ministry in the Church of Scotland vary widely, in practice team ministry in leadership of worship is slowly gaining ground, with a good deal of Old and New Testament sanction. The significance of this for our discussion lies in the use of different gifts, including the gift of an evangelist (which a minister may not have) in worship. The gifts of one particular minister are complemented by those of others, whether trained people like lay missionaries, readers or deaconesses, or those whose training is ongoing and informal.

In cities there are arguments for gatherings in different places and different times. In Edinburgh one congregation holds occasional outreach meetings in a pub across the road, and in Glasgow one pub has a regular Tuesday meeting which includes prayer and free debate about Bible passages. Traditionally, such gatherings should be for evangelism while worship would take place in the church on Sunday morning. But a clear distinction between the two is hard to maintain.

Imagine a contemporary open-air meeting. Gone are the days of a solitary preacher dressed in black with a faithful henchman at the back to give out tracts and tackle hecklers. Instead, a group of church members will be singing and worshipping God in the open air. Before morning worship at St Michael-le-Belfrey in York, a crowd gathers to watch drama and dance outside the building. This worship is part exposition of a Bible story or Christian doctrine, and part response to it. House groups likewise may combine worship and evangelism.

Much contemporary leadership of worship assumes a degree of teamwork between those ordained and not ordained. This is not in itself new but there is a new flexibility of roles, which poses questions over the meaning of ordination. This is not an argument for chaos in worship or outreach. The New Testament speaks of order, but it does not teach that one person (let alone a graduate!) will lead every prayer and preach every sermon. One mark of congregations which are experiencing renewal is the growth of worship teams not essentially different from the partnership of minister, elders, choir and organist, but certainly operating with greater freedom, expecting people to make a more immediate response to God, and often making more use of liturgical responses to give a shared backbone to worship.

Music, Drama and Dance

Another important area is music. The question of 'good' music tends to generate more heat than light, and musical snobs and illiterates have to co-exist. It seems that the Church of Scotland, in producing a supplement to the hymn book, and later a *new* hymn book, is finally accepting that new musical styles are not a passing phenomenon, and that the New Testament's 'psalms, hymns and spiritual songs' need not be strictly divided up between church and house group.

C S Lewis used to say that the unmusical must put up with 'good music', and the cultured put up with 'popular' music. To accept new music styles, amplified guitars, and so on, in church, is not simply an attempt to be relevant, it is quite simply to love one another, and to love the outsider. After all, it is the under-40s, not the under-20s, who belong to the age of the Beatles.

Jesus taught that the strong should serve the weak. In church worship, this means that those who are in a position of strength (often the middle-aged) must bend over backwards to accommodate the tastes of others (music hall style for the elderly, rock—and classical!— for the younger). And when those younger folk begin to gain power (as they will), *they* in turn have to start giving up what they want in favour of others.

Sometimes tension within a congregation over worship has simply to be faced and worked through. Love covers a great deal. Often God in his goodness provides 'a means of escape'. Folk music is one such means, as it is often acceptable to all ages; the Wildgoose worship group, for example, are currently providing such resources for the church. Another remarkable source of ideas, music and good theology are the three books published by Mayhew (Bury St Edmunds, 1986)— *Focus on Parish Music, Focus on Advent and Christmas,* and *Focus on Holy Week,* by G P Fitzpatrick and others. This is the most prolific (if not the greatest) age of hymn writing in English there has ever been.

The Netherbow Arts Centre in Edinburgh also offers music and drama resources for worship. Drama is a traditional way of illustrating Bible stories, and as such can form part of the teaching ministry within worship, as well as an ideal part of open-air worship which is often more accessible to outsiders. However, worship can never be simply a means to an end, even a worthy end like evangelism. Worship is for God, and tends to be most effective in reaching and converting outsiders when the congregation is caught up in God, and God in turn speaks powerfully to the congregation.

Drama is perhaps most effective when it is used to pose questions, to

give a new angle on an issue. It naturally accompanies a sermon which
includes biblical teaching relevant to the issue in question. But it needs
to be done well not to interrupt the flow of worship.

Dance, on the other hand, is part of the ministry of leading response
in worship. It too can be used simply to illustrate Bible stories (Springs
Dance Company have a memorable interpretation of Daniel's three
friends standing up to Nebuchadnezzar), but it is an appropriate
medium to express praise, or contrition, and to encourage a congregation to love one another and to pray for others. Dance poses problems
if worshippers associate it with lust and frivolity, instead of beauty; in
such a context it may be inappropriate. There may have to be
unlearning of false ideas about the body if the arts are to have their
place in worship. Here children can help a congregation to apply more
widely the point Jesus made about them. Their simple use of dance
and drama in all-age worship can help adults to appreciate new ways of
worship.

Dennis Lennon has given this quotation: 'Praise is the primary form
of the communication of the gospel, the sheer enjoyment of the grace
of God in our lives—all other communication is an overflow of this,
the spread of its scent, affirming in appropriate ways, in various
situations, the content and delight of praising God'. If that is even
partly true, then evangelism and worship must belong together. And if
we continue to love one another, then our churches will be growing up,
instead of folding up or blowing up.

5

Bible-Teaching Ministry and Evangelism

It is a surprise to me to be asked to contribute to this book, since some might consider me to have abandoned evangelism almost 40 years ago for what we call our Bible-teaching ministry in Gilcomston South Church, Aberdeen. I need not say anything about the results of that ministry, except that there has been almost always a steady evangelism integrated with it, and it is this which so many, who seem prejudiced in favour of overt and often self-conscious evangelistic activity, seem to discard and discredit. In particular, if one is thinking of the quality of one's converts, who not only 'go on with the Lord', as the saying goes, but become fruitful servants of the Lord, there is no doubt that such a biblical ministry—provided it is watered by the corporate prayers of the local congregation, which are quite essential—yields its own distinctive if not unique fruit.

Therefore, in considering the task of evangelism, I must gear the subject to that aspect of it relative to such a ministry. And if I do so, the stress I would want to put upon it is that of what I call 'primary evangelism'. To do so, I want to draw, not so much from personal experience of a Bible-teaching ministry, but from the biblical pattern of God's methods of evangelism as seen in the Scriptures of the Old and New Testaments.

It is clear that the intention of the Lord in calling Israel as his special people was not to favour them as an essentially superior race, but to be his evangelists to the Gentile nations. His method was perfectly simple, and gained some success and indeed ascendancy in the reigns of David and Solomon. If this is accepted, it is also plain that God did not want to make the people of Israel his *travelling* evangelists— Israel's long sojourns abroad towards the West in Egypt and the East in Babylon were her own fault—but God wished Israel to live the life of grace lovingly obeying the law of God so that she would prosper in her own land and thus draw the attention and envy of the surrounding

50

pagan nations to her superior way of life. When Israel was at her most prosperous, she certainly did that; in Solomon's day practically all the monarchs in the Middle East came to see not only the splendour of his court, but his wisdom.

This, I would maintain, is still God's purpose for Israel, and I believe the Almighty will yet hold her to it, as will be seen when the apostle Paul's prediction in Romans chapters 9–11 (but particularly 11) is fulfilled, and Israel is converted to Christ and draws the wondering eyes of the world to her.

Of course, because of Israel's failure to be the Lord's evangelists to the Gentile world, that plan was temporarily abandoned, and a new one, although still part of the old purpose, was instituted with the coming of Christ and his Church. Here the command is to go into all the world and preach the gospel to every creature. This was not entirely absent in Old Testament times as is seen from the Lord's command to Jonah. But now, there is this most pointed and all-inclusive command, which we disobey at our peril. This, I must confess, has often made me tremble when I have thought that in our day a pattern of long, settled ministries has prevailed, concerning which it would be easy to allege that the last thing that we do is to go into all the world and preach the gospel. Rather, we adamantly sit where we are and go on steadfastly with our Bible teaching, fervently hoping that this will do the task for us!

However, the answer to that, and it is often an abundant answer, and many men in Scotland and beyond would testify to it to their own surprise, is that the anointed ministry of the Word of God when watered by corporate prayer not only brings douce Kirk members to Christ, but often inspires them to leave everything to follow Christ, and sometimes to the very ends of the earth. The number of men and women in middle life and older whom I have seen abandon all to fill out their days in extensive evangelism in other places and other lands is one of the features of a long ministry.

As indicated, the command during the gospel day is to go into all the world and preach the gospel. However, it is nonetheless the firm intention of the Lord that, when the time comes to return to his original purpose of drawing the eyes of the heathen world to Christ by converting Israel to himself and making her shine gloriously and prosperously, people will come from the ends of the earth to see this great sight, a burning Israel aflame for God.

Now the application of this pattern of primary evangelism—shining for Christ where one is set—is to be seen when, by the preaching of the whole Word of God, church people in particular are drawn to the

Lord. And being built up in their faith, they go out into the everyday
world of their daily employment and amongst their neighbours to live
the Christian life there. Thus they attract others to the Christ in them
as their total lives reflect the love and care of God for people's bodies
and souls. This, of course, does not preclude the paraphernalia of
evangelistic activity in local congregational missions with door-to-
door visitation, or area missions or national campaigns. Since, however, there is inherent in special events something temporary, they can
easily lead to a life which is merely perpetuated but not advanced by a
series of boosts, rather than to a pattern of life which flows on
fruitfully, as the Word is allowed to do its gracious saving and
sanctifying work in the souls of men and women sitting under its
benign influence.

I therefore make no plea for the abandonment of other overt and
extrovert forms of evangelism, but for prior recognition that, underlying all such activist forms of evangelism, there is this fundamental
biblical pattern of building people up in their most holy faith and
looking to them to shine where they are. And then, if the Lord wills, it
sends them out into all the world to preach the gospel.

A rejoinder which can easily be made to those who see a steady,
consistent, Bible-teaching ministry as inimical to evangelism, is to say
that such a ministry not only produces converts who last—it also
produces evangelists!

II
Outreach to the
Parish and Community

1

City-Centre Lunch-Hour Services

My vision to reach out to people at their place of work came largely through the example of the Revd Dick Lucas, the Rector of St Helen's, Bishopsgate, in the City of London, who through preaching and teaching ministry regularly reaches hundreds of businessmen at his Thursday lunch-time services. I remember arriving at 1.10pm on a Thursday, accompanying hundreds of men in pin-stripe suits into St Helen's and watching open-mouthed as they listened attentively to what the preacher had to say.

That vision was further strengthened when I went to work as an evangelist in a city-centre church in the West End of London—All Souls, Langham Place. One of my jobs was to build up the very small amount of lunch-time work. Over the years there I came to see the strategic importance of reaching people at their places of work. We have begun to attempt the same kind of thing in central Edinburgh.

Special Opportunities

A ministry of evangelism in this setting has many advantages. First of all, working men and women often have free time during their lunch-hour—or can make free time if they find something they really want to fit in. Although the idea of going to a church service in the middle of a week-day may seem strange at first, it may even have its own novelty value as an attraction. People at work are open to peer-group influences (which are so powerful in Christian youth work) to an extent that will rarely be the case in their home situations. They may be much more likely to venture into a lunch-time service with a close colleague they know and respect, than they would be to go to their local church at home.

Lunch-hour services provide Christians with tailor-made opportunities to back up their personal witness to those they work alongside. The fact that they probably lives miles apart from each other may effectively restrict possibilities to the working day. Inviting a work-mate to your church on Sunday may be almost out of the question. On the other hand, someone whose home church is not very attractive—inward-looking, moribund, or just plain boring—may well be interested to try a church that takes its job seriously and seems to have some life to it.

There are other reasons why a mid-day service may draw in outsiders. By lunch-time people are still reasonably fresh and ready to make an effort to attend—which may not be the case at the end of the working day or the working week. Some will be lonely in the office, and responsive to a friendly invitation to a service that is welcoming without being intrusive and overwhelming. Others may be lost in the big city, and appreciative of a slot in the day that is reassuring and perhaps familiar.

The City for God

It is not only business people and shop assistants who are found in the city-centre at lunch-time. Shoppers, visitors of many kinds, holiday-makers, senior citizens breaking up the long day with the help of their bus passes, in some cities students and nurses—they all throng our city-centres in the middle of the day. Teaching and preaching the Christian faith in this context is a powerful symbol of God's claim upon the whole of life—the life and activities of the city where business is done, money is spent, things are bought and sold, and people pass much of their lifetimes—in an office or a bank or a shop. Christianity is not meant to be a hobby for those 'who like that kind of thing' in their spare time. If only in a small way, city-centre lunch-hour services are an attempt to affirm God's commitment to, and claim upon, the heart of city life.

What ingredients are needed to make this kind of activity work? I suggest the following:

The desire on behalf of a group of Christians to reach out to their workmates
You need first of all a group of people who genuinely want to reach out to their friends. This might at first be only a small group. If you have a nucleus of such people who will pray and work to make the service known, and befriend people coming to the services, then you have a beginning.

A church or building that is easy to get to
This needs to be preferably in the centre of the city, with close

proximity to people who work in offices. It does not have to be a church building, although using a church has many advantages. For one thing it is cheaper to run, as office rents will tend to be high in the city centre, although you do have the problem of heating, particularly in the winter. I personally like using the church itself. Many people feel safer if they are coming into a church building. But people used to centrally-heated offices will not come to a cold church. You cannot afford *not* to heat it!

A strong commitment to prayer
Ultimately it is prayer that will draw the outsider in, together with the right type of service and hard work. I suggest that the best thing is to call a lunch-time prayer meeting for the lunch-time ministry. Experience over the years has told me that a small rather than large group will come to this (perhaps a dozen or so). That does not matter, as long as regular, persistent prayer is made for the services. Prayer is a vital weapon if we are going to persuade busy people to give up their lunch-hours and come to a service.

A strong commitment to biblical preaching
What people are looking for is clear, simple, applied biblical preaching. They do not want high-sounding academic theology. They wish to hear and understand what the Bible has to say. So I have found over the years that the best approach is to work through the New Testament, or to look at a series of subjects arising from the Bible. For example, we studied Mark's Gospel over two years at All Souls and entitled it 'Question Mark'. In that way interest was maintained and people came eventually in their hundreds to hear what the Bible had to say. It always spoke to them at their point of need. I find it better too if the preacher is someone they know and trust and can build up a relationship with, although it is good to get in outside speakers to take the occasional series and add variety to what they are hearing. Above all the preaching must be interesting, otherwise people will not come.

The right kind of service
What are the marks of the right kind of service in this setting? I suggest that it needs to be *brief*—no more than twenty-five minutes maximum (we start at 1.10 pm and finish at 1.35 pm); it need to be *varied in content*—we usually follow the welcome and notices with a well-known hymn, a prayer, then the Lord's Prayer (which the congregation says together) and then finally the message, which usually gives the preacher 15–20 minutes; it needs to *finish on time*—people must know

that it is not going to go on after the stated time (visiting speakers need to have that stressed to them); it needs to have the *right atmosphere*—reverent but informal, friendly and contemporary, leaving you with the feeling, 'I wish it would go on longer'. And it must not be boring or irrelevant to the people coming.

Lunch following the service
This can be very simple and needs to be good value. (We find that soup and sandwiches and coffee with some fruit and biscuits are usually fine.) We charge for it and like to have the lunch available in the church itself so that people can stay on easily. The opportunity that lunch gives for fellowship and ordinary human contact is very important.

A programme that is outward-looking
It is very important that these lunch-hour services do not become inward-looking. We can keep them from becoming introverted in various ways. Special times of outreach can be arranged. The obvious times are Christmas and Easter, which lend themselves very well to special services. They are also times in the year when outsiders are much more likely to go to church. We can use evangelists from time to time, who will preach for a verdict and aim to call people to make a definite commitment to Christ. We should also encourage the members to advertise the services. A good publicity card giving details of what is offered is a great help and is worth the expense of printing, although we need to remember that publicity does not bring people in. People are brought, and won, by people, but invitation cards help people to bring others along.

The opportunities of lunch-time services are there for the taking. In many a town or city-centre they could be a significant avenue of Christian outreach. If they draw people in, they can provide a major new *raison d'être* for a church whose Sunday congregation makes it barely viable. We must by all means at all times seek to win our fellow citizens for Christ.

2

Outreach in the Inner City

I have been ministering in Glasgow's Inner East End for about five years, half of this period as assistant minister in Calton New with St Andrew's Church (and so, in effect, Leader of the Calton Youth Club), and half as minister of St Francis-in-the-East Church of Scotland in Bridgeton. In this chapter I share the thoughts and limited experience of someone who is still very much grappling with the challenge of the inner city. I hope that under God my contribution may prove helpful to others.

My parish used to be an area of urban decay, but in the last 15 years it has been largely rebuilt with most of the old buildings demolished and new ones built in their place. Even the remaining older buildings have been extensively renovated. However, it remains an area of priority treatment (an Urban Priority Area as defined in the Church of England's *Faith in the City* report) because, although the houses may be better, all the social evils of our day can be found in varying degrees within it. In addition to this, as a mainly working-class area, it shares in the traditional working-class reluctance to be involved in the church. I estimate that less than 5 per cent of my parishioners attend any church of any denomination. In such an area, there is a great need for evangelism, but the labourers are few—and the few we have tend not to be interested in participating in traditional patterns of evangelism. It is from such a situation that I write.

Church House

One of the most outstanding features of St Francis-in-the-East over many decades has been its attempt to build bridges to those outside the church, to provide half-way houses where both church folk and the unchurched feel happy to be, as a first step in our Christian outreach. The importance and value of this cannot be over-emphasised in an area such as ours. One of the most enduring examples of this is St Francis-in-the-East Church House. At the height of the Second World War a neighbouring parish church building closed through readjustment. Under the leadership of the Revd Arthur Gray, and with the support of the Presbytery of Glasgow and the Church's Home Board, St Francis-in-the-East converted this building into an open youth club. Since its opening in autumn 1942, thousands of young people from unchurched backgrounds have passed through the doors of Church House, and for a significant number, the work of Church House has led them to Christ. The present two full-time wardens of Church House are both living proof of this. Although such a project may seem too ambitious for some congregations (it is interesting, however, to note the recent rise in church-run open youth clubs in what had previously been shops or other suitable premises), many practical principles can be learned from Church House which I believe are of relevance to Christian outreach in the inner city.

Perhaps one of the most outstanding features of Church House is that, despite all the problems it has faced, including being at times without full-time leaders and having the inside of the building almost completely gutted and rebuilt, the work of Church House in almost 45 years has never stopped. Outwardly, the building and its activities may have changed over the years, but its work and message have never changed. And this dogged and consistent commitment is, I believe, a major principle in inner city evangelism. The people of my parish are all too used to new projects and new people coming in and starting up, and then in a few years' time disappearing. The past 40 years have seen unprecedented change in Glasgow's Inner East End. Apart from the institutions like the church, the schools and the DHSS, Church House is about the only project that has remained, and this stability, consistency and commitment are in themselves a remarkable witness to the unchanging God and his unchanging gospel. We now have in Church House, children who are the third generation of families who have come along to Church House, and each generation has found therein both positive activities and a genuine love, care and concern that have kept drawing them back. For, like God, we care for the whole person—body, mind and spirit—and in a culture that sees things concretely, rather than abstractly, and 'better felt than tell't', this is an important base for any Christian witness.

Arising out of this, there emerges another important practical principle: Church House is long-term Christian work done by the local church. It is not a 'short, sharp, shock treatment' approach to evangelism, which rarely seems to produce any lasting results in the inner city. Children can start coming to Church House as toddlers and have the opportunity to grow up there several nights every week (apart from the summer break). They find that the same people lead both the recreational activities and the spiritual activities, and, if needs be, discipline them. Most of these people also come, at least originally, from the children's own area and background, and so they understand them and can communicate with them. In such a situation, long-term nurturing can with time and prayer lead to people growing into Christ, and gospel seeds planted prayerfully in childhood can eventually blossom in adulthood. However, it is very important to realise that many also grow up in Church House with no sign of Christian commitment. (All we can do at the end of the day is leave our work in the hands of God for it is he who converts, not we.) However, even they frequently speak of the influence Church House has been on them, and a positive channel is often created and opened for future Christian witness.

Church House and Church

Nor is the work of Church House divorced from that of the local church. It has always been seen as part of the ongoing work of the local church, and many of its voluntary leaders come from our congregation. In fact, many of the leaders in Church House are also our church's Sunday School teachers for the 8–15 age group; and so there is a concrete link between church and club, a link which we also encourage between our other church-based youth organisations and the church. (In addition, all the youngsters are encouraged to stay in the church for the first half of our weekly Sunday service, until, halfway through the service, the creche and Sunday Schools begin.) However, despite such a link, many of the children who attend Church House are never seen in the church on a Sunday. Because of that, following a Summer Mission week in Church House, we started holding what the children have called the 'Bible Club' every Friday evening, a kind of grass-roots Sunday School based along similar lines to Summer Mission children's services, with choruses, quizzes, plays, arts and crafts activities, and stories all based on the Bible, communicating the Christian faith. Every Friday, between 40 and 60 children—most of whom are under 14 years of age and have been in a church only at a school service—come along to hear stories from the Bible, and some of them, after almost two years of attending the Bible Club, are now beginning to attend the church service on a Sunday of their own free will. We also hold what

we call the 'Youth Circle' for 12–18 year olds, again mainly from
Church House, on a Sunday night. This again has an overtly Christian
programme, yet around 16 teenagers come along to it. It started off in
Church House, but last September it started meeting in the church
instead, with no loss of impetus.

Incarnational Evangelism

The pattern that has emerged out of the development of Church
House is that of a long-term, incarnational approach to evangelism,
seeking to mobilise the Christians in the local church and parish to do
the majority of the outreach. Short, sharp raids from outside do not
seem to have much continuing effect in my parish; long-term, slow,
costly, getting-to-know-you, getting-alongside-you, incarnational
evangelism dealing with the whole person does. It is incarnational in
approach as it seeks to make our Christianity real and concrete, lived
out and not just spoken; but at the heart of it is the crucified and risen
Christ who alone can make all things new. In many ways it is more like
an overseas missionary approach than traditional parish ministry, and
maybe that is one of the reasons for its relative success. A traditional
parish ministry approach tends to be more suited to a middle-class
culture where people are more liable to think abstractly and verbally,
whereas the inner city tends to have a working-class culture in which
people see things more concretely and are less interested in words than
action. After all, they have been let down by words all too often before!
Getting to know the culture and outlook of the people in your parish
must surely be an important first step before trying to communicate
the gospel, and working-class Christians in an inner city church often
know and understand that particular culture and outlook far better
than a highly educated minister, because it is their background. This
poses two questions: to what extent, then, is the role of such a minister
first to nurture and train his people so that they can be released into the
parish as the local evangelists, and *second* to listen carefully to what his
Christian people say to him regarding effective patterns of evangelism
rather than to foist upon them the pattern that he thinks is best?

The Regnal

However, Church House is not the only area of evangelism undertaken
by St Francis-in-the-East. Another area which again basically follows
this incarnational, holistic approach is the men's Regnal Circle. The

Regnal League is a Methodist-based organisation that resulted out of
the experiences of a Methodist army chaplain in the trenches during
the First World War. As the Regnal League's admission ceremony
states, 'Regnal signifies the reign of Christ the King over the whole of
life. It follows, therefore, that its aim is Christian Discipleship'. Like
Church House, it seeks to develop and care for the whole person—
body, mind and spirit, and so its meetings are in three parts: (a) the
opening devotional, spiritual part, then (b) the mental activity,
whether it be a talk, a quiz or a discussion, followed after tea and
biscuits by (c) the physical activity, which can range from games to
church fabric repairs. For the first two parts of the meeting, all the
men sit in a circle and are encouraged to participate and treat each
other as of equal worth. Within the structure, there is plenty of room
for development. For example, in our circle the opening Bible reading
has been greatly appreciated. Because of the structure, activity and
depth of fellowship found in 'the Regnal', it has proved to be another
useful half-way house where both church folk and the unchurched feel
happy to be. Not only do many of my elders attend it, but also men
who would not otherwise have been inside the church, and through
Regnal over a number of years some men who might not have been
reached in other ways have been brought into the membership of the
church. There are presently four Regnal Circles in Scotland—at St
Francis-in-the-East, Burnside, Linwood and Wellpark West (all
Church of Scotland congregations)—each with their own particular
characteristics and emphases. If any reader would like any further
information regarding the Regnal League, I am sure that these circles
would be only too happy to be of help.

Another weekly evening meeting, which I started myself two years
ago, is what the people who first came to it have called 'One Step
Beyond'. It grew out of the Enquirers' Classes I run for anyone
interested in learning more about Jesus and the church, or who are
thinking about joining the church, or wanting to look again at the vows
they took on joining the church. At the end of one such series of
classes, which are very informal and participatory (scarcely classes)
over a cup of coffee, some of the new communicants asked if something
like this could continue—and so One Step Beyond began.

From the start, men and women aged from 17 to 70 have come, and
it now takes the form of a very informal, mid-week meeting to which
anyone can come when they like—and leave when they want to. It
opens with praise from *Mission Praise* (Marshall, Morgan and Scott,
1983). Then, after an opening prayer, we look at a Bible passage and
discuss what God is saying to us in it. Then we close with a time of

open prayer at which now, after two years of hard slog, people are beginning to pray aloud! This has never been a well-attended meeting, with an average attendance of only eight people, but over the last two years about 40 different people have attended it. Some have been church members, some have not. Some have come regularly, others have come for a few weeks then left. But again, it has proved to be a useful bridge to Christ and his Church for some, and it has been a tremendous source of Christian fellowship and spiritual encouragement to others not least to myself as minister. I know of some people who started coming regularly to our church on Sundays and eventually came to Christ only as a result of what they experienced in One Step Beyond. In addition, it has also helped to hold some new communicants once they have joined the church, and given them the opportunity to grow in the faith in Christian fellowship.

Our quarterly parish magazine *Challenge*, which usually has an evangelistic 'Message from the Manse' on its front page, is distributed to all the families represented in our local nursery and primary schools and our church organisations, as well as to our church members. I also take an annual Orange Lodge Service when the gospel is preached to many men and women whom I never see inside the church at any other time. However, some of our members are excellent at befriending folk, and through their friendship have brought people into the church. In these small ways, people have also been reached with the gospel.

Despite what this chapter might suggest, St Francis-in-the-East (now Bridgeton, St Francis-in-the-East Church of Scotland, after a recent union) is not a large, thriving, evangelical congregation. The number of people in it who are actually involved in evangelism is fairly small. The way forward for us must be to develop prayerfully what, and whom, we have, and to go out and reach others for Christ in these and other ways.

3

Mission in a Rural Community

With some variation of details the story has often been told of the missionary who went from the West to the East with the message of the Christian gospel. One day as he was preaching a listener interrupted him. 'That's a good tale,' he said, 'but I have a question. If what you say is true, why have I not heard of it before? Why did my father never hear this message and my grandfather before him? Surely if it were true, someone would have told my people long before now.'

The missionary was at a loss for an answer. At last he said, 'The Lord Jesus left orders with his Church to take this message everywhere. But the Church has been slow in doing it. You know how people are; they do not always do what they are told'. And with that the missionary went back to his preaching.

It was something in the sting of these words, 'If what you say is true, why have I not heard of it before?' which compelled the Kirk Session to give serious consideration to the Church's responsibility to get the gospel out to our entire community. Not that evangelistic outreach was something altogether new; a Children's Mission has been part of our church's programme every summer now for some years. However, little had recently been undertaken to reach out to our rural community of some 5000 souls.

Preliminary Reflections

There are several preliminary issues required to be thought through. To begin with, there was the conviction that our primary responsibility in terms of outreach should be to our own parish. In a world where half of the people have never heard the Good News in Jesus Christ, how are they ever going to hear if there is no witnessing Church among them? We as a Church, therefore, ought to be witnesses right here where God has put us. This particular concern for our own community influenced

C

our thinking at the earliest stages. It directed us away from the more traditional and elaborate type of evangelistic outreach whereby as many as possible would be invited to attend a large gathering conducted by the evangelist. Also, it was clear to us that for the Church in the Book of Acts, evangelism was something that involved everyone. The early Christians were often involved together, like fishermen pulling together on the same net. The Holy Spirit seems to have used the *community* of believers, the body of Christ, to perform that multiplication of Christ's work. Their witness together was powerful in the hands of the Holy Spirit. Therefore, we were particularly anxious to involve the whole congregation. Further, it might be a comparatively easy thing to enlist the support of neighbouring churches who would send their people along to fill the church for an evangelistic rally—and indeed, for us to find our church filled with the very people we did not want—the evangelised! However, it would be quite another matter to persuade those we did want—the unchurched—to attend a meeting in the kind of religious atmosphere in which many people feel very uncomfortable. Some other approach was clearly called for, which, in our rural situation, would involve the whole membership of the church.

As a result of these preliminary considerations, an approach was made to Christian Ministries, a team of three men based in Witney, Oxfordshire, with wide experience in church-based evangelism and Bible teaching, both in the UK and in many overseas countries, always with the one great aim of declaring 'God's Word for Today's World'. With the assistance of Christian Ministries, therefore, and some 18 months ahead of the projected dates of our mission, the planning began.

A steering committee was carefully chosen—not because of any particular evangelistic zeal, but rather as representative of the entire congregation. At this earliest stage it was decided to call an additional weekly prayer meeting especially for the mission. There was no need to ask God if we ought to evangelise—we are quite clearly commanded to do so—but there was a very real sense of the need to know the mind of God, that we might go about it in his way. And so, very early, we began to pray and to do so in earnest.

The Mission Takes Shape

Gradually it emerged that the general, overall direction of the mission would be along the lines of a whole series of meetings of a smaller nature, as many as would be possible during the nine-day duration—from the Saturday evening until the following Sunday. The task was clearly enormous. However, having accepted the biblical principle that while not all Christians are called to be evangelists, all Christians are called to be concerned and burdened about the unsaved—here was a glorious opportunity for the whole membership to show that concern. This they were urged to do. Members were invited and encouraged to use imagination and initiative in thinking out various groups of people within our community who could be brought together, both within the church itself—fortunately, there has never been any real feeling that our church buildings are 'consecrated' property that cannot be used for community outreach—and also within the home, in that very natural, ready-made situation where families within the congregation would be able to reach out to non-Christians.

The response by the congregation was most encouraging. Members opened their homes to unchurched neighbours, friends and others. Each hostess was responsible for inviting anywhere from 6 to 20 people, not chosen at random, but chosen prayerfully in the belief that God would lead to the right person. These house-meetings were scattered throughout the whole parish, and while they involved a great deal of prayer and hard work, they brought rich rewards in reaching non-Christians of all ages and backgrounds. As many as 26 such house-groups met within the course of the week, mainly in the mornings. After coffee, the evangelist was invited to speak, and lively discussion usually followed.

In contrast to these smaller, more informal house groups, it was possible to arrange a whole series of meetings within the premises of the church itself, once we had been able to identify groups with common interests. For example, lunches were held for local shop-keepers and tradesmen, police, schools' staff, senior citizens, a group of unemployed persons, doctors and health visitors. Suppers also were planned for parents, young couples, Guildswomen and their guests, and the over-twenties. An exclusive men's dinner brought together about 130 people, and around 30 golfers returned from an afternoon's competition to a dinner evening. The exact nature of the meetings was always made perfectly clear to those who were invited. There would be a meal perhaps, followed by an address by one of the evangelists on the relevance of the Christian faith for today. Teenage work as well was carefully threaded into the general mission programme. For young people a special Open House was held in a different home every evening, and as many as 30 attended nightly, in addition to the 200 and more who turned out to the larger teenage meetings arranged for the Saturday evenings at either end of the mission.

However, we were able also to go beyond the church premises and the homes of our members. Being the local parish church, the importance of a good standing in our community must be stressed. There are several things which account for this. To begin with, the church has always taken its role very seriously. Those who belong to the church are different. Church members are expected to fulfil their vows of membership—to turn out on the Lord's Day, to support the work of the church generously, to demonstrate the reality of their faith not just in the things that they do not do, but also in their prayerful and practical concern for the well-being of everyone within the parish. This distinctiveness is quite apparent: and our good reputation is further enhanced by the fact that church members are involved in the life of the community. They try to act as salt and as light in our society. We have some fine Christians in the local bowling club, to give but one example. Church members are seeking to be very much involved in the world while at the same time recognising that they are not of the world. In any rural community, such a witness does not go unnoticed. Therefore, wherever the church went during the mission, doors were open. Visits were welcomed by the management of the local factory, by the heads of the four local schools, as well as by the committee of the bowling club. These were to prove invaluable openings.

In total, 59 different meetings were organised and, with a great readiness, people accepted the personal invitation extended to them. The only notable exception to this was at the local factory. Although lunch had been provided in the canteen, and the whole workforce— about 90 men—were invited to remain afterwards to hear the evangelist (in extra time kindly granted by the management) only one man remained to listen! The evangelist was not unduly dismayed, and spent much of that afternoon going around the factory talking to the men individually and distributing Christian literature. However, it was a salutary reminder to all of us that this world is not the friend of grace nor of God.

Such a large-scale programme packed into a matter of nine days, and undertaken by a comparatively small and very ordinary, rural congregation, may have seemed too great an undertaking. It is perfectly true that we were stretched to the limits of our resources. On not a few occasions we needed to remind ourselves that whilst our resources might be limited, God's were not. In the area of finance, for example, we did not face the major problem that many anticipated— not because we had plenty, but because God provided what we required. And so again, amongst the many unforgettable lessons, we proved, as so many have done before, 'that God's work done in God's way never lacks God's resources'. Apart from all that was involved in the house groups and young people's meetings, the church gatherings alone required the provision of some 800 suppers, 500 lunches and 160 dinners—all provided free, and prepared and served by the ladies of the congregation.

The importance of prayer could never be overstated. Without doubt, one of the great strengths of the Church of Scotland is that we are able to share with, and call upon the help of, others of like mind. That we did unashamedly and unreservedly! The result was that throughout the Church in Scotland people were praying for us—many of whom had never before even heard of us. The sheer encouragement of a number of fellow-ministers, as the mission itself grew near, was a source of unforgettable blessing. Regular prayer within the congregation's life had been established at the very outset. However, one of the most fruitful suggestions made was that of a full week of prayer immediately prior to the mission, and leading straight into it. In fact, it was during the early hours of a morning, in the course of this prayer vigil, that one person praying actually came to faith, before the mission had ever begun, thereby setting a wonderful seal on all that was to follow in the days ahead. This intensity and earnestness of prayer were maintained throughout the mission: prayer cells were formed, and such was the burden of concern, that during every one of the meetings held, a group of praying people were at work behind the scenes to bear that particular gathering—the people and the evangelist—before the throne of God's grace.

Despite the large number of meetings, and the wide variety of people who attended, two important features marked them all. *First*, there was the message. The sheer wealth of their experience and the obvious passion for their calling resulted in the three evangelists using their God-given abilities to present the gospel in a simple, clear and natural way. No-one was ever in any doubt but that he or she was being confronted with the real issues of life; and that this was clearly a most serious matter. *Second*, there was the hearing which attended such a message. People did not only come; they listened, and they listened intently. There was a great openness; and, of course, many people were actually hearing the gospel for the very first time. Significantly, these two features had been among the main burdens of our praying over the many months. The format of the meetings was kept deliberately simple. No singing of hymns or any other preliminaries were involved. People were welcomed, the meal was served, the gospel was preached. Then on leaving, and having been given the opportunity to speak personally with the evangelist, each was given a letter from the Kirk

Session thanking him for his attendance, a list of the church's activities together with a warm invitation to attend, and a copy of John Blanchard's book *Right with God* (Banner of Truth Trust, Edinburgh), one of the finest and most straightforward books ever written for those searching for personal faith in God. Almost 1000 copies of this book were thus freely distributed.

Assessing the Outcome

The assessing of results is never easy, and perhaps the simplest thing that can be said is that we saw happening exactly what we expected. As mentioned, people listened. Many of these people came to faith and are going on in that faith. Perhaps even more came to an assurance of their faith. And we find this to be of great significance. Perhaps because of the very structures of our congregational life, even in a rural situation, it is almost impossible to get to know one another intimately. Thus, it became clear that there were many people who were already converted, but for whom there had been little opportunity previously to give expression to their faith. These people in particular found the mission to be a source of great blessing and encouragement. Of course, there were many others who came, and who left just as they had come: they have not been back since. And again, there were a few who appeared very enthusiastic, who came along on more than one occasion, spoke with the evangelist, and showed great promise. They came to worship and even to the mid-week meeting for Bible study and prayer. But, alas, they only lasted for a few months; and today they are no more. In other words, we saw happening exactly what our Lord said would happen whenever his gospel was proclaimed.

The effects upon the church itself were quite fascinating. It was made very clear by the evangelists at the outset that one of the aims of their coming was not so much to evangelise the community, as to make the church evangelistic. No-one was ever left with the impression that being involved in this particular week of outreach would fulfil his evangelistic obligations for the next decade! The result is that the church today is quite different. There is far greater openness to speak about the gospel and about spiritual things—even in the wider community. Worship, prayer, Bible study and outreach have assumed their rightful places in the lives of a great many more people and take precedence over everything else in our congregational life. Elders, leaders and ordinary members are much more concerned that we should be the church in our community. And after all, is this not precisely what the church is all about? Can there be any greater disobedience than a church squandering its resources on itself, and refusing to live and die on behalf of a world for whom Jesus Christ gave his life? We do not exist for ourselves either as a local congregation or indeed, as a particular denomination. As the apostle Peter reminds us, 'You are a chosen race, the King's priests, the holy nation, God's own people'—why?—that you may declare the wonderful deeds of him who 'called you out of darkness into his own marvellous light' (1 Peter 2:9, GNB).

So there is a new awareness of our calling, as well as a new openness to spiritual things. However, there is also a new, holy boldness. Of course, we approached the whole mission as the apostle Paul approached the Church at Corinth—'in weakness and fear, and with much trembling' (1 Corinthians 2:3, NIV). But if there is any one lesson which we learned, perhaps even more than all the others, it is this: that God honours and blesses the obedience of his people. God never asks us to go it alone, to serve him in our own strength. He is with us. And as such, he has given us the greatest possible assurance of success.

There is a statue in the grounds of a church in Boston of Phillips Brooks, one of the city's great preachers. It is in the form of a canopy, in which there are two figures. The first is Phillips Brooks, dressed in his robes. One hand is up, the other is holding a Bible. He is proclaiming the unsearchable riches of Christ by which multitudes came to know the Lord under his ministry. Further back under the canopy, there is the other figure, of Jesus. But unless you look closely, you will not even see this other figure, because it is dark under that canopy. Jesus has his hand upon the shoulder of Brooks as he is preaching.

And that same presence of the one who said, 'All authority in heaven and on earth has been given to me. Therefore go and make disciples of all nations . . . . And surely I will be with you always, to the very end of the age' (Matthew 28:18–20, NIV), was our very real experience too; because it is a promise which our Lord gave to every one of his servants. He promises to be with us always: to be with us in our congregations as we undertake missions; to be with us in our families as we make this a priority; to be with us in our personal lives as we do it. And that is why it is very little wonder that this congregation of the Church of Scotland, set within its rural community, will never be quite the same again. Among all of the lessons we have learned, we have discovered at a new and a deeper level that Jesus has the authority; he had told us what to do; and he has given the greatest possible assurance of success.

4

Personal Evangelism in the Parish

Every Christian, although not always aware of the fact, possesses God-given gifts and talents which can be dedicated to Christ and developed in the service of his Church (see Ephesians 4:7–13).

After I committed my life to Christ at the age of 17, like so many other young Christians I felt a compulsion to tell others what Christ had done for me. Over the years that followed, at school, college or university, I continued to do what seemed to me quite natural, and endeavoured to introduce others to Christ. Eventually, under the guidance of the Holy Spirit, I came to realise that God's gift to me was that of communicating the gospel through personal evangelism.

Although I have attended many courses of instruction in evangelism I still look back to the 1940s, when, with the Church of Scotland Evangelist, the late D P Thomson, I worked on successive summer missions throughout the length and breadth of Scotland. To that great man of God I am indebted for an invaluable practical training in personal evangelism.

Jesus and the Woman of Samaria

In John chapter 4 we find the wonderful record of Christ's encounter with the woman of Samaria. In company with many teachers and evangelists, I have always felt that the natural sequence of events in that narrative is illustrative of the finest evangelistic method. Perhaps one of the best analyses of that method is given by Dr D James Kennedy in his book, *Evangelism Explosion* (Tyndale House Publishers, Wheaton, Illinois, 1980). He first reminds us that:

The modern witness for Christ should never lose sight of the statement of the Apostle Paul: 'Whoever does not have the Spirit cannot receive the gifts that come from God's Spirit. Such a person does not understand them; they are nonsense to him because their value can be judged only on a spiritual basis' (I Corinthians 2:14, GNB).

The witness should be taught from the very beginning to depend not on his own persuasiveness but upon the power of the Holy Spirit; or else he is witnessing in the flesh and not in the Spirit.

Introducing his discussion on guidelines for communication Dr Kennedy writes:

Someone has well said, 'You can't sell the gospel; in fact most Christians can't even give it away'. This illustrates two truths: one, there is something involved far beyond salesmanship, namely, the supernatural work of the Holy Spirit, and two, from the human standpoint most Christians need a better understanding of how to sensitively communicate the gospel conversationally and persuasively.

Discussing Jesus' use of the five laws of persuasion, Dr Kennedy continues:

There are five principles of communication: attention, interest, desire, conviction, and acceptance. It does not matter whether you are selling a refrigerator or persuading men to accept a new idea or philosophy, the same basic principles hold true. Did salesmen invent these? No, they just extracted them. They learned that this is the way that the human mind works and reaches conclusions and takes action. This is what Jesus did, for example, with the woman at the well (in John chapter 4).

This can be summarised as follows:

Attention
Jesus began where the woman was and attracted her attention by asking her for a drink of water, even though traditionally Jews did not associate with Samaritans.

Interest
He gained her interest by speaking about living water. This roused her curiosity and made her question the source of this living water.

Desire
She requested what Christ was offering, but for a selfish reason. She was a woman of ill reputation and had to go to the well at noon when no-one else was there. Others came to the well in the cool of the day. She thought this living water which Jesus offered would conclude these weary and lonely visits to the well.

Conviction
Jesus put his finger on her sin by speaking of her previous husbands and present life-style. She tried to avoid the issue by raising the argument between Jews and Samaritans about where God should be worshipped.

Acceptance
Jesus used something from her digression to get back to the main subject and confront her with the decision she must make. He did this by claiming to be the Messiah she had referred to. She was now confronted with the living Christ. She must either accept or reject him.

What a wonderful testimony the Samaritan woman had that day when she ran into the village of Sychar and through the market place, shouting, 'Come and see the man who told me everything I have ever done. Could he be the Messiah?' (John 4:29, GNB).

Visitation

During the first few years of my ministry in Edinburgh, my visiting was confined to members of the church who lived within the parish bounds and beyond. Then I felt a need to visit every home in the parish and, with the help of a team of young people from St Ninian's, Crieff, and members of the congregation, this was done. Record cards were made out for each household with details of the members, and the dates of birth of children for Sunday School purposes.

In addition to this valuable exercise a number of parish missions were undertaken by student mission teams working in conjunction with the Youth Fellowship, by the Faith Mission, and by volunteers from St Ninian's. Despite these efforts, and weeks of special services and a variety of guest speakers, our church, in common with many others, had been experiencing a gradual decline in membership and I had become concerned that I could be at fault and failing the Lord in my ministry.

In the spring of 1983 I spent a month in hospital, which gave me an extended opportunity to think and to pray. I became convinced that a programme of visitation evangelism was God's plan for the parish and felt assured that God would be with me and my co-workers in going out with the gospel, and that people would be brought into the kingdom. So it was to prove.

In Christ's unique encounter with the woman of Samaria almost

2000 years ago, we have seen the application of the basic principles of effective communication. How could we, in a parish situation today, follow the Master's example in dealing with the people we meet?

With the help of a few dedicated Christians, we began a programme of parish visitation, to be repeated in succeeding years. I have always felt it best to begin visitation evangelism in the spring, in order to cover the area before people go off on holiday.

Week by week at our Church Bible Study and Prayer Meeting we prayed that God would move the hearts of the people in the 1700 homes to be visited. Calling at each of these homes, we would introduce ourselves, talk with the people, and leave them a letter greeting them in the name of the Church of Jesus Christ and welcoming them to worship in the Parish Church.

Responses

The vast majority of people indicated that they were not interested in the Church or in Christianity, but, thank God, there were the few who once were church members, who were anxious to come back to fellowship with God's people and did, in fact, do so.

Generally, my fellow-workers in the gospel were free only in the evenings, but I was usually able to visit four afternoons per week, and on some evenings. In this way I was able myself to visit 1000 or more homes.

Initially, we used 'There is Hope' material, which included a broadsheet and a reply card (available from PO Box 158, Brunswick Road, Edinburgh EH7 5YA). We contacted those who returned the cards, and I recall visiting a widower of about 60 years old who spoke in loving terms of his late wife who was a fine Christian. He had not been a member of any Church but was anxious to become a Christian. I read a portion of God's Word, prayed, left with him literature I always carry with me—*Directions, Journey into Life, The Way Ahead*—and promised to return. On my next visit I discovered with joy that he had read the literature prayerfully and had committed his life to Christ.

Subsequently, members of the congregation have been visiting one half of the parish and I have been visiting the other half, changing around each year. More and more I am convinced of the need for prayer in every household and so I pray as I walk from one door to the other.

Many of the best opportunities for evangelism occur quite naturally in everyday settings—a bus queue, a railway carriage, shopping, walking round the parish, stopping to talk to someone in the garden, someone washing a car, workmen digging in the street. Let there be no barriers. Jesus made a simple request of the Samaritan woman—'Give me a drink'. One must take time to speak to people and, having established contact, go on talking. Many people want to talk and all of them are souls for whom Christ died. We must let the love of Christ reach them through us.

When going round the parish I am addressed as Minister, Padre and, frequently, as Father. I wear the clerical collar at all times and do not have to waste time explaining who I am. One day, in answer to the bell, a door was opened and an elderly man said, 'Come away in, Padre'. After a long and interesting conversation it transpired that both he and his wife had been members of the Church of Scotland. As I bade them farewell the man said, 'I will be at church on Sunday'. He was, and the following Sunday his wife was with him. Since then, both have been faithful attenders, rejoicing in worship and Christian fellowship, which can be clearly seen in their faces.

On another occasion, having been warmly welcomed into the home of two senior citizens, I felt very strongly that the Lord wanted these dear people back in the fellowship of the Church, and I prayed often that this might come about. On a subsequent visit they produced Communion cards 25 years out of date, and they, too, decided to come to church.

One day, getting no reply at the door of a bungalow, I called to make enquiries at the neighbouring house. I learned from the lady of the house that she had once been a member of the Church and would love to return. Meantime, the lady of the first house had returned home. She was of like mind, and so was her neighbour in a third house. The following Sunday all three were in church. Some months later one the three said to me, 'I am so glad you found me'. I was glad that the Saviour had found her.

Young and Old

An interesting feature of visitation evangelism is that over the past four years 100 people of the older age group and 38 of the teenage and early twenties age group have been brought into the fellowship of the Church.

A girl in her early teens was converted in the vestry one day, and so rapid was her growth in the Christian faith that, within a year, she was leading the Youth Fellowship. There is no limit to what God can do in a young life.

A lad of 17 approached me and indicated his desire to become a Christian. We talked, and I made plain to him the way of salvation. The seeking sinner and the seeking Saviour always meet: the lad was on my prayer list and I trusted God to answer prayer. The boy came to see me in the vestry one evening and when I asked him how he was progressing, he said: 'I was praying last Tuesday night and I felt my prayers were not being heard and I said, "Lord, if you hear me, wake me at 3 am". I awoke close to three o'clock and said, "Thank you, Lord, take my life."' The lad would not have heard of Gideon's fleece, but he put God to the test and God heard and answered.

During the course of pastoral ministry there may be little evidence that our contacts have led to conversions, but in faith and in the power of the Holy Spirit we continue to reach people with the good news.

Many courses of training in evangelism are undertaken in our cities, at St Ninian's, Crieff, and at Carberry Tower, Musselburgh, and we should avail ourselves of all the facilities provided. (I have also derived great help from books on evangelism by George Dempster, John Stott, D P Thomson, David Watson and Maurice Wood. Norman Warren's booklets are useful in presenting the gospel simply and concisely.) In the last analysis, however, whatever is achieved will only be through prayer, the power of the Holy Spirit, and the presence of God with us at every door and in every home.

5

Church Extension Opportunities

Conscious of its missionary responsibility to the whole nation, for over a century and a half the Church of Scotland has given a high priority to the work of Church Extension. The beginnings can be traced back to 1828, when the General Assembly, moved by a concern for the ever growing number of people in a rapidly expanding industrial society who were completely unchurched, appointed a Committee to look into 'The inadequate state of Church accommodation in many of the large towns, manufacturing villages and populous Parishes of the country'. Six years later, this Committee, which had been re-appointed annually, was established in a permanent form as 'The Committee on Church Extension'.

A large-scale church-building programme followed the appointment of Thomas Chalmers as Convener of the Church Extension Committee in 1835. 'Inspired by the gigantic evil of the unevangelised masses, Thomas Chalmers threw himself into the task of Church Extension,' wrote Professor G D Henderson, 'and was the means of erecting in the course of seven years more than two hundred churches at a cost of over £300,000'.

Another major contribution to the cause of Church Extension was made by the Free Church of Scotland, which came into being as a result of the Disruption in 1843, Thomas Chalmers being its first Moderator. 'In two years no fewer than 500 churches were built,' G D Henderson tells us—an astonishing achievement, made possible by the evangelical zeal and sacrificial giving of the members of the Free Church.

Add to their efforts the continuing commitment of the Established Church to the work of Church Extension, in building mission churches and establishing mission stations, and also the considerable number of church buildings erected by the United Presbyterian Church, from 1847 onwards, and it becomes clear that a very different situation existed at the end of the nineteenth century from that which had, rightly, caused so much concern 70 years earlier.

But the population of Scotland continued to grow, and then, in the years between the two World Wars, a great movement of the population took place as large housing schemes were built to replace run-down slum properties in inner-city areas. This constituted a serious challenge to the Churches, both Established and United Free. Thus, in 1930, the Church Extension Committee reported to the General Assembly of the newly re-united Church of Scotland: 'Such has been the rapidity of the movement for the housing of the people, and the extent to which various schemes have been forwarded during the last decade, that the Churches, occupied as they have been with domestic questions, have failed to keep pace with the demands of the newly populated areas'.

Soon a fresh impetus to the work of Church Extension was to be given by the strong leadership of Dr John White. Between 1932 and 1940, 21 complete sets of buildings and 17 church halls were erected, and a further 11 projects were begun. The years following the Second World War saw an even faster rate of progress. A massive house building programme included the construction of Scotland's five New Towns and a number of very large housing schemes. During this period nearly 250 church buildings of varying type were completed. At one stage a new church or hall was being opened every month.

Those were great days for Church Extension. As a report to one General Assembly put it:

> Without buildings of substance or tradition, the Church in the new Communities has had to start again with nothing to offer men and women but the Gospel, and in the open air and crowded living rooms, and school classrooms, and Contractors' huts, in all kinds of so-called 'secular' surroundings, the Gospel has been declared with a new simplicity and directness.

If it were not for the major contribution made by Church Extension to the mission of the Church of Scotland over the last century and a half, the Church of the 1980s, committed to a National Strategy for Evangelism based on its parishes, would surely be seriously handicapped.

Church Extension opportunities are missionary opportunities. The work of Church Extension is front-line evangelism. It was this conviction which drew me to two widely different Church Extension situations—Townhead, Coatbridge, and the New Town of East

Kilbride. It is to the story of Claremont Parish Church, East Kilbride, that I turn first.

The policy of the National Church Extension Committee is to co-operate with the local Presbytery in the creation of a new parish, when it becomes clear that a need for one exists, and then to appoint a minister, as soon as possible after people have begun to move into the area. Thus, in April, 1968, when my induction to Claremont took place, our new parish, which would eventually have a population of some 12 000, consisted of many acres of farmland, a former golf course, and a number of extremely muddy building sites, reached by equally muddy and rutted roads. A few rows of houses had been completed and were occupied by some brave pioneers, while many more houses and blocks of flats were under construction.

Prior to my induction, Bill Black of *Life and Work* helped us prepare a publicity leaflet for use in our first efforts in outreach. He produced a most attractive design with a bold statement printed across it— 'The church is here too!' And so it was, even though that church, numbering a dozen or so people, met for worship in the home of a recently arrived family from Glasgow.

A congregation which begins like that—rooted in and identified with a new community from a very early stage in its development, is strategically placed to commend the gospel to the people of its parish in a way that few other congregations can ever hope to be. But if this unique opportunity for evangelism is to be exploited to the full, it is imperative that a carefully planned programme of outreach is set in motion without delay. In the strategy which we devised, each newly let house received a leaflet from the church, delivered to arrive along with all the advertising material left by local tradesmen, so that it would be found when the tenants opened the front door for the first time. Then, armed with a list of names and addresses supplied by the Development Corporation, the assistant minister or myself would visit each house, usually within a matter of days of its being occupied. Members of the church were enlisted to help with the follow-up care and encouragement of those who showed interest or needed some kind of practical help, but that initial visit was invariably made by one of the ministers, and this, I am convinced, was immensely important. It meant that we knew and were known by the people very quickly indeed. Relationships were established with whole families. The committed Christians were discovered—and put to work! Lapsed Church members who produced 'lines' yellow with age were encouraged to make a new beginning, while others, who, back in their old environment, would never have darkened a kirk door, responded to our invitation. Communicants classes were large, and made up of folk of all ages, some in their sixties and seventies.

At the end of the first year, Claremont's Communion roll contained some 350 names. Dr Andrew Herron, preaching at our first anniversary service, remarked that he could see little difference between this one year old congregation and that to which he had ministered in the historic kirk at Houston, except, perhaps, that our time of service was 2.30 pm, and our place of worship a Roman Catholic school hall. A year later, the membership was 600, and, by the time we moved into our own premises, just before the church's third anniversary, it had reached almost 1000. This growth continued until the membership stabilised, in the region of 1500. The Sunday School was started in 1968 with 90 children who had been attracted by means of a Summer Holiday Mission held in a marquee. Five years later it numbered 700. A wide range of organisations were opened up during that first year, meeting in a variety of borrowed or rented premises, and, miraculously the necessary leadership was always available. I am convinced that the Lord sent us the people *he* had prepared to start the Sunday School, to take charge of the organisations, and to form our Kirk Session; men and women deeply committed to Christ and with a wealth of experience and a real sense of being called to serve in this challenging and demanding situation. Add to all this a congregation developing quickly into a warm and caring fellowship with a clear awareness of its missionary responsibility towards the parish, and one could only say: 'To God be the glory, Great things he has done'.

But not every Church Extension story is a success story. Some new congregations have never grown strong enough, in terms of leadership and a committed membership, to make an effective evangelistic outreach to their community. A variety of good reasons can be found to account for this: the social mix of the population, the proportion of Roman Catholics to Protestants in the parish, the proximity of the nearest town or city, are some obvious factors. The difference in growth rate and ultimate potential between a New Town parish and one situated in a housing scheme has often been noted. If that housing scheme is located so near to the place from which its people came that they can conveniently travel back to their existing church, experience shows that many will do just that, so robbing the Church Extension congregation of leadership and support which would have been invaluable.

Townhead Parish Church, Coatbridge, to which I was inducted in 1958 suffered from this—and other disadvantages. The congregation dates from 1950, a hall church was built in 1954, and the parish with a population of some 7000, about 50 per cent being Roman Catholic, is situated a mile and a half away from Coatbridge Town Centre. When I arrived, the church membership was over 600 and there was a real spirit of expectancy and hope for the future in evidence. But the problem which had to be tackled was how best to mobilise this congregation for mission. The impact of the recent All Scotland Crusade had been real, and several of our members owed their conversion to it. It was through a close working partnership with Tom Allan and his congregation at St George's Tron in Glasgow, as they continued so effectively in this work of evangelism, that we found the encouragement we needed to embark on mission in our own situation.

Some years prior to moving to Coatbridge, I had been introduced to Tom Allan, and now there came an invitation to join a group of ministers from the greater Glasgow area who met with him each week for Bible study, prayer and the planning of various projects in mission. Soon a number of our young people from Townhead—and some older folk too—started coming with me to the monthly Evangelistic Rallies in St George's Tron. On one never-to-be-forgotten Saturday, as Tom Allan made the appeal, while the great congregation sang 'Just as I am', all the young people from Coatbridge rose from their seats and went forward together. That marked a turning point in our Youth Work. We now had a band of enthusiastic young Christians who were ready and willing to become involved in the life of the church with a wholly new commitment, and who formed the nucleus of a Seaside Mission Team the very next summer.

But we had still to tackle the task of mission to our parish. Although by now the church was growing in numbers, and in the range of its activities, we were still not reaching the people right outside our influence. Obviously we must go to them. But how could we set about it? Most of our members were shy and diffident about sharing their faith, and anyway it would be a massive undertaking, seemingly beyond our ability to organise. There appeared to be no solution until, one day, Tom Allan suggested that our congregation, assisted by some of his own members, might consider holding a mission to the parish under his leadership. Sadly Tom suffered his first heart attack in December 1961 and he was unable to take part. But the mission went ahead, as a joint enterprise, in April, 1962, supported by that group of ministers who shared so fully in Tom's evangelistic work, and who now rallied to help us.

Each evening of the first week, a team of members from St George's Tron arrived for a meal at Townhead Church, where they were joined by an equal number of our own members. After prayer and briefing they went out in pairs—a Townhead member with a 'seasoned campaigner' who would take the lead and cope with the difficult situations. Amazingly they managed to cover the entire parish, visiting 1636 homes on the five evenings. So we achieved, in partnership, what we could not have accomplished by ourselves. That week of outreach was followed by a well-supported preaching mission, and soon we were busy calling on the many contacts which had been made, one of these being with a couple whose marriage and family life were transformed because our visitors came to their door and spoke to them about Christ. When, within a couple of years, the husband died, one of his workmates told me how everyone who knew him recognised the change which came into Robert's life after his conversion, and how he kept a Bible in the cabin of the crane he drove.

Twenty-five years have elapsed since that Parish Mission, so it is good to find Townhead Church featured in *Ten Growing Churches* (edited by Eddie Gibbs, 1984). The chapter by Peter Bisset, Warden of St Ninian's, Crieff, who was involved in the Mission of 1962, brings the story up to date. 'There is little doubt', he writes, 'that the congregation presently is rejoicing in the surge of new life and vitality which has carried them forward into a new experience of hopefulness.'

Church Extension opportunities are missionary opportunities!

6

Parish-Based Mission

Rather than compile an anthology of styles of parish-based mission, a sort of stamp collection of bright ideas, I want to describe the way in which one congregation has wrestled with the task. The specific events mentioned are therefore relevant to St Thomas's situation in West Edinburgh, but the approach to the task will, I believe, prove to be useful in other places. We undertook a programme which committed us to six major faith-sharing events, of between 10 and 14 days each, in the space of three years. At the end of that time God had given us the growth and spiritual confidence to send out some 70 members of our congregation to plant a new church in the centre of Edinburgh, a work which is having a great impact on the part of the city.

Not so much a Parachute Drop as Working in the Fields

It is important to have a sound model for parish-based mission. Much evangelistic endeavour, particularly of the Crusade type, resembles what the Pentagon calls a 'vertical insertion', *ie* a parachute drop. People are taken off to hear the preaching at the mega-event. Or a group of skilled communicators arrive in the parish, take the lead, do the communicating, assemble a list of decisions and depart. Then, so often, the parish heaves a sigh of relief and returns to normal.

If, on the other hand, our model is of the parish as farm land for which we are responsible before God, our approach will be radically different. We shall then steadily attend to the work of preparing the land, ploughing, sowing and looking to reap. Like a farmer we will learn to trust the mysterious energies of the seed when it takes hold, the hidden work of germination, and the need to be patient and consistent in our work. Of course the visiting speakers have a proper and valued place within this scheme of things, but they will always be people we invite in to join with us in our work of mission. Notice also, that with this agricultural model the work is always going on but with right timing. Sometimes the work is simply the steady demonstration of Christ's love on the part of the congregation through visiting and caring; sometimes it is shown by striking examples of divine power through healings at many levels. Then come the times for more public and intensive activity as well as more urgent prayer as the congregation plans to engage with the parish in evangelism. God willing, there follows the time when new life appears in the fields. Like the delighted farmer in the parable we are pleased to acknowledge that, 'the seed should sprout and grow, [we] know not how' (Mark 4:26–29, RSV). Neither do we know which particular event, or ministry, or individuals in the Church were used by God to cause the seed of his word to take hold in people's lives. It would be more accurate to say that it is the total ministry of service, prayer, love and witness, throughout the year, which is used to bring new life to the parish.

Attitudes

For a church to engage realistically in parish mission requires a certain attitude within that church. In practice this means that the entire or even the majority of the congregation will seldom share the attitude to the same degree. The leaders, the wise people in the congregation, the people of faith and vision, must agree, and then work to communicate the vision to the rest of the congregation through painstaking explanation and discussion. The essential, fundamental attitude is that your church *faces outward* towards the outside world and not inwards in self-indulgent church activities. Leaders should encourage and initiate the groups and activities which do this. It will mean that groups in the church should regularly review the outward-facing orientation of their life. Are your people making and developing friendships? Is the church a part of the answer in that it helps people make new contacts, or is it a part of the problem in that its programme becomes a lock-up for members? For example, if a church is taking its mission to the parish seriously, what will this mean for the shape, ethos and language used in the Sunday services? We have found that many of the traditional/contemporary conflicts relating to worship can be settled if we ask the question, 'Would this make sense to the newcomers we are trying to reach?' Given that the church is committed to its mission locally, many of these intractable problems do yield and progress is possible.

Setting up a Pattern for Parish Mission

Let us assume that a church is open to God and wants to win its parish to Christ. It is the responsibility of the leadership to work out a pattern and framework within which the congregation can share its faith. Assume also that there is a steady, consistent effort to engage with the outside world through the existing groups and organisations. From this point my own church moved into more high-profile mission in the following ways.

We dropped the word 'mission' with its connotation of one-off, once-in-a-blue-moon, big-bang event which leaves the church exhausted. We used the low-key word, 'faith-sharing', and aimed for two faith-sharing events, called Breath of Spring and Autumn Gold, each year for three years initially. Four ingredients would be essential—*relevance, integrity, attractiveness* and a dash of *celebration.*

Relevance
Relevant to whom? *First,* to the soft fringe of people with nominal faith, people who generally look favourably upon the church, folk who have connections through youth organisations, marriage, baptisms, funerals, and so on; *second,* to the friends of church members wherever they live, in the parish or outside; and *third,* to the untouched and unreached homes in the parish. We take as our master-idea Paul's experience at Athens (Acts 17). He preached the straight gospel (vv 16–18) and was mis-heard, misunderstood and misrepresented, an experience we know well today. So he said it all over again but this time he took his text from their culture. He surveyed the art and architecture of Athens and seized on the cry for help in the altar to the unknown god (v 23). Using their own poets (v 28) he engaged their attention and led them through to think about Jesus (v 31). In our culture people do not go around asking about the 'unknown god' but seem to be preoccupied with the 'unknown man'. To be relevant, therefore, to people in our culture is to meet them at the point of their concern about their lives and lead them through to Christ. It means we must tackle the issues which worry them, we must demonstrate our own ability as Christians to enjoy life and in particular show that we value warm friendship and fellowship.

Here then is the outline of our parish faith-sharing event, Breath of Spring. Is it relevant to people concerned about their own lives and the 'altar to the unknown man'? It is organised over two weeks and consists of the following:

Come to the Ceilidh! (Have fun and friendship.)

'AIDS—a blessing in disguise?' A lecture by a Christian Professor of Medicine which will lead people to consider the purpose for which God has made us. Held at the local College of Education.

Supper Party in a local home using the video 'Silent Witness' about the Turin Shroud.

Guest Service on Sunday in church.

Supper Party in a local home for young parents on the theme, 'What's happening to our kids in school?' with a local Christian teacher speaking.

Supper Party in a local home at which several young Christians will speak about their experience of Christ.

'A loving God in a world of pain?' A theologian, a Christian Professor of Oncology, and a Christian who has recently passed through a severe illness, speak about their faith in God in the midst of pain and suffering. Held at the local College of Education.

'Wine and Cheese' at a local hotel to meet and hear a well-known Christian TV Communicator and author answer the question, 'Why am I a Christian?'

For men, supper in a local pub and a talk from an evangelist.

Youth Barbecue *etc.*

Final Sunday Guest Service.

Each event is organised by a different group in the church. The two lecture events—on AIDS and on suffering—will attract some 200 people each time. Tucked in around these main events are numerous coffee mornings, video parties in homes, and so on.

We feel that for our district this programme is sufficiently locked-in to people's concerns (for example, AIDS, education, suffering, personal spiritual experience) to appeal to them as realistic.

Integrity
Because this type of programme is offered every six months, there can be no suggestion of high-pressure salesmanship, or of a shallow 'Jesus is the answer-ism'. He is indeed the answer and he is worthy of an intelligent, satisfying representation in terms of people's anxieties about their existence. The word will get around the parish that, yes, these things are worth going to and, no, they do not twist your arm to 'decide for Christ'.

Attractiveness
The programme must be attractive in the straightforward human sense of the word. Notice that only the Ceilidh and the Sunday Guest

Services take place on the church premises. Everything else happens in homes, hotels, or using the excellent facilities of the local College of Education. Notice too the stress on entertaining, hospitality and, indeed, on eating together!

Celebration
The programme proves enjoyable and profitable for the church members also. They can take pride in the gospel presented in this way. On other occasions, as time and resources may allow, there has been more in the way of musical contributions. But so often the gospel concert approach can be *very* expensive and *very* time and energy consuming. It needs to be very good, and in our experience very little results from it! But the deciding principle here is what is relevant to your parish. And so, three weeks before Breath of Spring (or in September, Autumn Gold), our own outreach paper advertising the events goes into 11 000 local homes.

But what about the Decisions?

If the programme is too low-key evangelistically it may simply evaporate into pleasant gatherings and conversations. If it is too aggressive it will touch only the small number ready to turn to Christ at that moment, and tend to slam the door on the many people who are feeling their way towards the Lord. This Breath of Spring and Autumn Gold programme does, obviously, have its forthright evangelism. But we have learned to shift the burden of calling for a decision off the events in the programme (except for the two evangelistic Guest Services) onto the follow-up course, called Brass Tacks.

At each and every event and gathering throughout the programme (excluding the Ceilidh and youth events) people are introduced to Brass Tacks and invited to join the course. It starts immediately after Breath of Spring and runs for five weeks, one session a week. We say it is of value to longstanding church members who may want a refresher course in basic Christian faith and experience, to the new convert, to the disillusioned spiritual drop-out who would like another look at Christianity, and so on. 'Whosoever will may come' to Brass Tacks. The theme of the course is the new covenant God makes with us in Christ by the Holy Spirit. A blend of teaching and discussion enables people to see what the basic Christian faith and experience really are and how to come into them. This, in fact, is where the evangelism takes place.

Increasingly we feel that the appeal to people around the parish is

'Are you now ready to start to learn what life in Christ is all about?' Large numbers of Christians now in our church had the beginnings of a confident faith in Christ in Brass Tacks. Because it is an integral part of the outreach to the parish it stands like a net at the end of Breath of Spring. All kinds of people (not only those who have been converted in the events) are able to come through to the course and deal with their doubts and questions. In this way we lift the burden of decision-making off the specific events in the outreach and we trust the seed of God's Word to work. Here, surely, is the aim of mission to the parish—however we do it, we want to bring people through to the place where they are reading God's Word with a seeking mind. The rest is up to God.

The indirect evangelism of many of the events in a programme such as Breath of Spring acts rather like Jesus' parables. They engage people's attention and curiosity and act as a bridge allowing them to move nearer to the truth and to the challenge of the gospel.

III
Partnership Between
Churches in Mission

1

Presbytery-Wide Mission

In recent years the General Assembly of the Church of Scotland has begun to put a new stress on mission and evangelism. This was reflected in the report *Urgent Call to the Kirk* which was presented to the Assembly of 1983 by a group of senior churchmen. In 1984 the Assembly approved the report *Towards a National Programme for Evangelism* and instructed Presbyteries to respond to it. Other reports and initiatives followed in subsequent months.

It was in the context of this mounting concern from the Assembly that the Presbytery of Lochaber's Ministry and Mission committee met in October 1984 to consider the report *Towards a National Programme for Evangelism*. The convener suggested that the Presbytery should engage in evangelism by planning a Presbytery-wide mission. Both the general outline and the detailed scheme were accepted by the committee and subsequently by the Presbytery. Thus what came to be called 'Lochaber Mission '86' was born.

General Outline

The aims of the mission were stated as follows:

1 To declare the gospel of the saving grace of God in Christ Jesus.
2 To call men and women and young people to faith, repentance, obedience and service.
3 To encourage commitment to Christ and his Church.
4 To teach responsible discipleship.
5 To demonstrate the unity of the Church in the proclamation of the gospel.

The programme for the mission was to fall into four phases: (a) the initial period from November 1984 until the beginning of 1986, a time to determine strategy and tactics, to train people, and to make the work known; (b) the preparatory period of four weeks immediately prior to the actual mission when we would deliver literature to every house and generally mobilise our congregations; (c) the mission itself, from 16 February until 16 March (Easter Sunday); and (d) the follow-up period.

Having looked at the planning stages and seen the conception of the project, we must now leap forward two years and report on what actually happened. The best way to do this is to consider the various parts of the mission.

Training

Training was given to those who would be involved in any one of a number of areas. There were general training days for the Mission '86 Committees which were set up in every parish. We trained house group leaders and set up house groups in every parish during the preparatory period. Over 450 people attended one or more of these. We trained people in visiting and in personal evangelism, those who were to be involved in children's mission, and those who were to be running bookstalls. There was even some training for film projectionists to ensure that this important work was not done in an amateurish way.

In all of this training we involved the people from outside Lochaber who were responsible for particular areas of the mission.

Personnel

Lochaber is a small Presbytery and with peculiar problems. It covers 2000 square miles and much of it is accessible only by single track roads and some of it only by sea! There are about 10 000 homes in the Presbytery area and they are scattered in some remote places as well as in urban Fort William. We recognised that to carry out effective mission in such an area it would be necessary to bring in to help us people with gifts and expertise which we could not produce from among our own number. The following were of great help:

Speakers
Dick Dowsett of the Overseas Missionary Fellowship and Stephen Anderson, the Evangelist with the Church of Scotland, were our principal speakers. Mr Dowsett's main responsibility was the nightly meetings in Fort William which were intended to be the focal point of

the mission. Captain Anderson worked mainly in the outlying areas
with his 'Scotroc' music and drama team.

House Groups
Brian Burden, one of the training officers based at St Ninian's, Crieff,
prepared material for the house groups and came to Fort William to
train those who would lead the groups.

Film Festival
This was essentially the brainchild of Mr Bill Morrison, the Deputy
Secretary and Director of Publicity for the Church of Scotland. He
introduced us to Bob Spratt of International Films who co-ordinated
the project. Mr Spratt both trained people and was also present for the
two weeks of mission when the film festival took place.

During the mission there were over 40 showings of various Christian films. In particular, the film 'Jesus', still on premier release basis,
was made available to us.

Children's Work
Derek Hobson of Scripture Union co-ordinated the work among the
children. Each parish was offered a one week mission for children.
Personnel was provided and trained by Mr Hobson. Ultimately there
were 14 such missions attracting 500 children.

Student Team
Bill Taylor of St Ninian's, Crieff, recruited and brought to Lochaber
two teams of students who visited in 13 parishes and generally helped
wherever they were needed.

Literature
Stewart Anderson, a representative for a number of Christian publishing companies and an elder of the Church of Scotland, masterminded
the difficult task of arranging for a bookstall in every parish and
training someone to operate it. He also liaised with the Church of
Scotland bookshop in Glasgow which supplied everything we needed.
Mr Anderson recommended certain books which we particularly
promoted as being of some relevance to the situation of mission and
evangelism. About £1300 worth of books were sold.

Gospel and Handbook

The National Bible Society of Scotland arranged for a specially printed edition of Luke's Gospel in the Good News Version. This was bound in with the *Journey into Life* leaflet and had a tear-out slip for further contact or information. The front and back covers were designed specifically for Mission '86 with our logo, a photograph of Ben Nevis(!) and some information about the mission. The NBSS gave us these at cost price and we bought 10 000.

We also produced a handbook which gave details of every parish in the Presbytery: times of service, organisations and so on, together with a day-to-day programme for the two weeks of mission. This was introduced by a letter from Alan Ramsay, the Moderator of the Presbytery, and a statement of the gospel.

The handbook and the gospel went to every home in Lochaber (at least that was the intention). This meant that every home received the Word of God as a gift and also received an invitation to the various Mission '86 meetings. Logistically this was the most difficult part of the whole operation; in terms of future results the gospel in every home must be seen as perhaps the most significant achievement.

Prayer

Every Presbytery was asked by the General Assembly to appoint a Prayer Correspondent whose responsibility would be to encourage and stimulate informed prayer at every level. Lochaber Presbytery took up this suggestion in specific relation to the mission. Thus John Maitland, an elder, was appointed Prayer Correspondent and he produced Mission '86 prayer letters every eight weeks for almost 18 months. Prayer meetings were to be held in every parish every eight weeks especially for the mission and prayers used in Sunday worship with the same frequency.

From the beginning the committee made clear its view that prayer was the key to mission. Our job as Christians is to present the gospel faithfully, but only God can save, only God can forgive sins, only God can grant the new birth.

The Congregations

Although outsiders were brought in to help as leaders in specialised areas of ministry, it was always believed that the main work would be done by the congregations. If the members of the congregations were not mobilised and prepared, then the mission would be a failure. It must be emphasised that people were brought in to help, not to 'do mission' on our behalf.

Inevitably, some were more committed to evangelism than others. Both the time of mission itself and the time since would, if assessed objectively, lead to the conclusion that those congregations which put most into Mission '86, received most in return. In some cases this was growth, in others a recovery of enthusiasm and joy, and in others still a real rededication to God.

The level of involvement and commitment expected of congregations is revealed in the statistic that in two weeks, in 16 parishes, there were over 100 meetings! If anyone in Lochaber did not know about Mission '86 it was not for the want of trying.

From the beginning it was understood that this was to be a mission planned and carried out by the Presbytery of Lochaber as a specific response to General Assembly reports, suggestions and encouragement. Nevertheless, we were happy that a number of our friends in the other denominations felt able to support the mission. Indeed, one member of the Presbytery's Mission '86 committee was appointed for the sole task of liaison with other Churches.

The Programme—and its Cost

We have touched upon some of the events which took place during Mission '86 in what has been said above, but let us go quickly through the list: services and meetings with speakers; films; youth nights with the student teams; literature evenings (book parties!); barbecues; gospel rock concerts (with the band 'Triumph'); drama and music with Scotroc; children's missions; visitations; house groups; an evangelistic musical; and fellowship evenings; we also went into schools, pubs, factories; and individual congregations planned some events of their own as well.

Clearly, all of this was very expensive. The Christian Film Festival cost somewhere in the region of £1500, the Gospels about £1900. Indeed, the whole budget was around £7000. For a small Presbytery to meet this target was remarkable in itself.

A levy was imposed upon each congregation, and larger donations were invited from congregations. This brought in around £2000. We also received about £5000 in grants from various sources, including very generous help from the Congregational Mission Fund of the Department of Ministry and Mission.

We obtained help with individual parts of the mission too. One company supplied all the paper required for printing 10 000 handbooks. Another gave a donation towards the Film Festival, and so on. One of the lessons we learned was that money is available for all kinds of projects from all kinds of sources!

D

Conclusions

The above has been very factual and no apology must be made for that, since the best way to discuss Presbytery-wide mission is to report on one example of it. Nevertheless, it has not been possible to convey the ethos and atmosphere of Mission '86. They were exciting days and full of expectancy. I can vouch for that personally. To have dealt properly with Mission '86 and all its ramifications and results would have been a book in itself rather than a chapter. We can, however, draw some conclusions and make some comments.

When Klaus Buwert, the convener of the Mission '86 follow-up committee, presented his committee's assessment of Mission '86, it included the words, 'On the whole the return for so much effort seems small'. In terms of conversions that is true. His concluding words, however, are more positive and I share their sentiments: 'The Mission was a worthwhile exercise, from which much experience has been gained, many lessons have been learned, and perhaps some pointers to the future have been given. The Church of Scotland in general will benefit much by studying this Mission'.

Lochaber Mission '86 was unique, partly as the first example in Scotland (as far as I am aware) of a Presbytery of the Church of Scotland engaging in a co-ordinated outreach campaign of this nature. It was also unique in its scale. Any one aspect of the Mission would have been significant on its own (500 children attending SU Missions!) but when it all came together it was a truly remarkable achievement.

Above all, however, Mission '86 affected those who were involved in it. For about 18 months evangelism was on the agenda of every Presbytery meeting, and was sometimes the main item. It was in our conversations and in our prayers. Indeed we might say that Mission '86 contained an element of self-destruction. In other words, it generated a spirit, an enthusiasm and a dedication which, if nurtured, would render such missions unnecessary—for then our whole lives and the lives of our churches would centre upon God, and evangelism would be our daily task, and our joy.

2

Town-Wide Mission

'You in your small corner, and I in mine.'

Having ministered in Falkirk for some eight years I was aware that even among evangelical Christians in the town there was little coming and going. We acknowledged one another and made intimations of certain events, but there was no joint action in outreach.

I became aware of the need for mission in our own town, and made contact with Dr Alastair Noble, a member of the Christian Brethren, and suggested that we should give thought to a mission in our home town of Falkirk. He readily agreed, and with a small group of Christians we further discussed and prayed over the matter and decided to invite Christian leaders of all Protestant denominations to a meeting held in one of the local hotels.

That was in the spring of 1981. A good representation of the churches and missions in the district met on a Saturday morning. The proposal of a year long mission was put, and after much discussion and many questions, it was agreed by the majority present that this venture should be taken up. We were ready to come out of our own small corners and band together for the cause of Christ and his kingdom.

Baptists and Brethren, Apostolic, Nazarene, Pentecostal, Methodists and Missions, Salvation Army and Presbyterians were all represented on the Committee which was formed, and it can now be said that the bond that was formed at that time between fellow Christians was one of the great blessings and enrichments which came out of Reach Forth '82.

The year of mission on which we embarked was to be known by that name—Reach Forth '82. In the Central Region of Scotland we live by the River Forth, and these words were meaningful in the light of Christ's command to go into all the world and preach the gospel. So we banded together to Reach Forth with the good news, and though it had

its beginnings in 1981, its climax would be reached in 1982.
Here is a timetable of events:

1981   Autumn: weekly prayer meeting.
        October (to March 1982): Callendar Park lectures.
        Winter: 17 house groups began.
        December: pre-Christmas open-air meetings.
1982   April to June: additional monthly prayer meeting.
        May to June: open-air meetings.
        June: 10 day mission to secondary schools.
        June: after-church rallies.
        July: distribution of gospels and booklets.
        August: children's meetings in housing schemes.
                10 day Crusade meetings.
                Home coffee meetings during Crusade.
                Lunch-time open-air meetings during Crusade.
        Winter (to spring 1983): lectures on the Prophets.
1983   Further series of open-air meetings.

The outreach was two-fold. *First*, it was to bring Christians together
in fellowship and service, and to instruct and equip them to share their
faith with others. *Second*, it was to proclaim the good news of God's
love and forgiveness through the Lord Jesus Christ to those who were
not Christians.

Prayer

From the outset we were aware of the immensity of the task on which
we were embarking, and knew that only by looking to and leaning
upon God could we see it through. Prayer therefore was essential and
not only in the individual's private prayer life. Time was set aside in all
committee meetings when we brought all our plans before the Lord,
and there were times when we would break off from our discussions in
particular matters to seek the Lord's guidance. In the autumn of 1981
a weekly prayer meeting, which was to continue regularly through the
year of mission, was held in St Andrew's Church every Wednesday
morning from 7.30 am to 8.30 am. In April, May and June there were
further monthly meetings of prayer from 10.00 pm to 2.00 am; and
during the ten days of Crusade Meetings in August 1982, a prayer
meeting was held each morning from 8.00 am to 9.00 am. Prayer
bookmarks were printed giving dates and times of meetings and also
details of matters which required particular prayer. Although much

prayer was offered, the prayer meetings did not get the support which one would have expected from professing evangelical Christians.

The Callendar Park Lectures were one of the great blessings of that year long campaign. A series of talks on basic Christian beliefs was given between October and March by well-known evangelical ministers in the lecture theatre of Callendar Park College of Education. On the whole they were reasonably well attended. Recordings were made of each lecture and these sold well. The series was based on the theme of 'I believe'—in the Bible, in God, Sin, the Ten Commandments, Jesus Christ, Miracles, the Cross, the Resurrection, the Holy Spirit and the Second Coming. Opportunity was given for questions after each lecture, and also for informal discussion over refreshments in the College Dining Hall. This further time for fellowship proved to be a great blessing, and a place where Christians from different denominations had the opportunity to get to know one another.

House groups were also a feature of Reach Forth '82. A seminar was led by Captain Stephen Anderson. This was a profitable and enlightening time for the 100 or so people who attended. During the year 17 groups met throughout Falkirk and the district. The group size varied but it was decided not to have a group numbering more than 15. Preparation meetings were held for those who were to lead the groups in studying St John's Gospel. Some 170 people met in these groups, learning the truths of the faith, and being challenged to live and apply the gospel in their daily life.

Open-air work was seen as an essential part of the mission. Permission was granted by the local authorities to hold open-air meetings by the Steeple in the High Street of Falkirk on Saturday afternoons, when the street was crowded with shoppers. One of the local shops provided the electric power for the microphones and other instruments which are prominent in present day Open-Air Witness. Four meetings were held leading up to Christmas. There was good musical presentation, and opportunity for witness and short gospel messages. In May and June, there were open-air meetings on Saturday afternoons. During Crusade Meetings in August, lunch-time meetings were held through the week and on Saturday afternoons. It is known that some people were converted directly or indirectly through Open-Air Witness. Indeed, one whole family was reached through the message in song. Many gospel tracts were handed out—some 10 000 with a message relevant to the Soccer World Cup which was being held at that time! If there is a good presentation, and prayerful preparation, the Open-Air Witness has still a place in present day evangelism and can arrest the attention of people of all ages to listen at least for a short time.

Reaching the Young

The outreach to teenagers and school children was given an important place in Reach Forth. A ten day mission in June to secondary schools and coffee bars was led by Stephen Anderson and the Scotroc team. Opportunities were given to reach the young people in schools, meeting them on their own ground in their classrooms, also in assemblies and lunch-time concerts. Coffee bars were held in the evenings—at first on so-called neutral ground, in a café in the town, for example—but to our surprise, the best attended and more successful coffee bars were held in a church hall! A good hearing was given to the gospel message in all these places. One teacher was reported as saying, 'The Scotroc visits to schools are to be warmly commended for their impact upon the pupils and for the sincerity and courtesy of the team'.

Permission was also sought from Head teachers in Primary Schools, and two members of the committee who had been involved with children's work—one a primary teacher—met with children of Primary 6 and 7 classes. Special children's meetings were also held in two of the large housing schemes of the town in the month of August prior to the Crusade meetings.

Thus the Word of God was made known to many hundreds of young people by various means—songs, drama, testimony, teaching and preaching; and God has said, 'My word . . . shall not return unto me void' (Isaiah 55:11, AV).

The National Bible Society of Scotland was very helpful when approached about the distribution of the Gospels throughout the town. Some 20 000 copies of St John with *Journey into Life* attached were bound in a cover with the Reach Forth logo, and a word of introduction and invitation to the Crusade meetings was also printed on the cover. A copy went into every home in Falkirk (population around 40 000) and also to some of the villages in the surrounding area. About 200 persons were involved in the distribution of this literature during the month of July, prior to the Crusade meetings which were held in August.

Crusade

Leading up to the Crusade, 'After-Church Rallies' took place on Sunday evenings during the month of June. Guest preachers from different denominations were invited to share in these services, which were arranged to encourage Christians to prepare themselves further for the part each was expected to play. Women's coffee meetings were also held before and during the Crusade. Homes were opened and neighbours and friends were invited to share a time of friendship over a cup of coffee. During the morning, opportunity was there to speak of the Crusade, and to speak about Christ. Three Counselling classes were held to prepare those Christians who had been commended by their church or fellowship to do this work. Navigators material was used, and also in the counselling pack there was a copy of St John's Gospel with a Scripture Union study plan and *Journey into Life*. Counselling arrangements at the time of the Crusade could have been more efficient, and lessons were learned here. Publicity too had its part to play all along—keeping people informed by *Reach Forth News*, prayer cards, information concerning the 'I Believe' lectures, and then immediately prior to the ten day Crusade, posters of various sizes were placed at strategic points in the town including libraries, Employment Departments and factory floors. Good coverage was given by local newspapers and radio network, and the RAC had 50 signs in position leading into the town; and within the town the RAC directed cars, buses, *etc*, to the Crusade meeting place, which was Falkirk Town Hall for eight days, and St Andrew's Church for the closing two days.

The Crusade meetings were led by members of the committee. The choir was trained and conducted by a local leader, and the evangelist was Dr Alastair Noble. The only imports for the meetings were the musical group, from Northern Ireland, and the soloist, a local man who had been working for many years in another part of Scotland. On the first night the attendance was around 500 and night by night it increased, so that on the last evening the Town Hall was packed with 1000 people. On the closing night in St Andrew's Church, which seats around 900, every seat was occupied and there was an overflow to the hall where people shared in the rally by closed-circuit TV.

Each evening after the meeting, tea was served in another hall, and there people mingled together sharing fellowship, and talking with those who wanted to find out more about Christ. A large bookstall was in a prominent place with an excellent display, so that many had the opportunity to browse and buy Christian literature and music.

Some might say that the visible response at the time of the Crusade was disappointing, but we know that one soul is precious in the sight of the Lord. Of those who sought counselling, 25 were known to have accepted Christ as their Saviour, 6 found renewed assurance and 13 rededicated their lives. These persons were put in touch with the ministers or leaders of the churches; the Christians who counselled also kept in touch and sought to give them spiritual help and encouragement in their early Christian life.

During the winter and spring following the Crusade a further series of lectures were given on the theme, 'The Prophets Speak Today'. Like the Callendar Park Lectures these ministries were much appreciated and were a source of great spiritual benefit. Open-air meetings also continued the next spring and summer. Thus the outreach was not restricted to the Crusade meetings alone, but had an impact beforehand and afterwards.

Did someone ask what it cost? It cost much in many ways—time, energy, talents—and there were discouragements. But were we not doing it for One who said 'If anyone wants to come with me . . . he must forget himself, carry his cross, and follow me' (Mark 8:34, GNB)? In cash terms all expenses involved amounted to just over £9000 and at the end of the Crusade every expense had been met, and a small surplus was in hand.

We could only say, 'The Lord hath done great things for us; whereof we are glad' (Psalm 126:3, AV) and thank him for the privilege of service to the town and community where he had set us to act as his witnesses. Eternity alone will reveal what was accomplished in the town mission of Reach Forth '82.

3

Festivals of Faith

In a roundabout way the General Assembly is responsible for Festivals of Faith. At the 1982 Assembly, a call went out for a National Day of Prayer and Repentance, and, in response to that call, a number of Church of Scotland ministers in the south side of Glasgow arranged a Sunday evening of prayer from 8.00 pm until midnight. To our surprise, almost 500 people attended and shared in the time of guided open prayer.

A few days later, a small group of ministers who had been meeting regularly for two years to support and pray for each other felt the time had come to act. A day was set aside for prayer and planning, in which they diagnosed some of the current ills of the church in their area. There was an underlying conviction that evangelism needed a renewed Church if we were to make the message of Jesus real to the people of our generation. Areas of felt need were listed and noted:

(1) A new spirit of worship which welcomed some of the new music which God was giving to his Church, and allowed room for other creative expressions of worship and communication.

(2) New opportunities for fellowship to allow people to build one another in faith.

(3) A wide range of teaching topics according to spiritual stage and inclination rather than the age-bands of normal church life. We needed to offer teaching for the seeker, the young Christian, and for the mature Christian to help him relate his faith to family, daily work, his life in the church, and the big questions of the contemporary world.

(4) A context in which whole families could worship and feel at home, and the family of God could meet without regard to age.

(5) A new focus for evangelism in the ongoing life of the local church.

The idea was conceived as a mutual help scheme, whereby each minister would host an event in his own church with the other ministers attending to assist in the teaching, and pooling the resources of music, drama or other talents from the respective congregations. One event would be held each month in a different church for a year— and then a review. Festivals of Faith were born.

Format

The format of the original Festivals were based on the following needs diagnosed:

Worship with praise, both ancient and modern, for about 40 minutes.

Workshops on a wide variety of themes for an hour.

Tea or juice provided, with a bookstall on occasion; a place for people to meet.

Closing worship with a challenge.

Opportunity for counselling as required—either by retiring to a private room, or as later developed, a time of prayer ministry and counselling at the end of the evening in a very open-ended way.

The fact that it was a mobile Festival meant that the host minister was responsible for organising the event once a year, and the host congregation had the benefit of experiencing joyful worship in a packed church on a Saturday evening. The queues were the best advertising you could want!

The format of Festivals in other parts of the country has varied according to the local situation, but many have operated on a similar style. Others have aimed at a large central venue for a combined event which was more worship and less teaching. Some have even been adventurous enough to stage the event outdoors!

Workshops

The teaching workshops have been a vital element in the Festivals as they were originally conceived. 'Grace Invaders' for the children has meant that families can come and worship together. Titles for other workshops have been as varied as 'The Authority of Scripture', 'Sex and the Single Christian', 'Resurrection on Trial,' 'God on the Dole,' 'Infant Baptism,' 'The Nuclear Debate,' and 'How can I find God?' Sometimes they ran in a series, such as 'Kirkspeak' on the major reports of the previous year's General Assembly, or 'The Letters of Paul' giving historical and thematic overviews of the main letters of the apostle.

There was always a workshop for the seeker on the simple basics of the faith and the fundamental questions that need to be dealt with on the way to faith. People opted to be evangelised! It also meant that Christians could bring their friends and know that, as well as enjoying the joyful atmosphere of worship, they could attend a workshop which would be at their level.

Some of the pastoral workshops on marriage, divorce, healing, childlessness, sexuality and bereavement, were greatly valued. They provided opportunities for pastoral ministry and also for training for elders and other carers.

A later development led to adopting a smaller number of themes and continuing them throughout the winter, more as a training scheme than as a one-off talk on a topic of interest. The training focussed on Ephesians 4:11—prophets, evangelists, pastors and teachers—helping people to listen to God, to share their faith, to be more effective in pastoral care and to teach the Word of God in a life-giving way

In this way the church in the area was built up for Spirit-directed service and ongoing personal evangelism.

Leadership

The quality of the Festival will be related to the fellowship base of the leaders. One of the needs of the Church today is to rediscover the New Testament model of shared leadership which is more than simply an organising committee.

This kind of leadership means being open and vulnerable to each other. It means praying together, as well as planning. It may even mean time spent in retreat to discover the next step of the Spirit's guidance. Evenings spent together in times of fun and laughter over a meal are equally important in the process of building a fellowship for leading the people forward.

It may be that the kind of model worked out in such situations provides the basis for other areas of leadership in Kirk Sessions and Presbyteries.

The Value of Festivals

The value of such Festivals might be gauged in terms of numbers. The Glasgow Festivals rose from 350 to over 1000 people meeting on a Saturday night. They must have been meeting at least some of the needs of the people at that time. They might be judged by the compliment of copying which was paid by so many other areas of the country. They might even be judged in terms of the number of people who came to Christ through these events, and there are considerable numbers of people who responded to the opportunity to receive Christ on these evenings.

However, the value of the Festivals of Faith lies in the fact that they were really Festivals of Hope. At a time when many Christians felt defeated and discouraged, they provided a ministry of encouragement. At a time when many felt frustrated and confined by cramping traditionalism, the Saturday night event was free to happen without any limitations of the expectations surrounding the Sunday morning service. They provided a place to which Christians could bring uncommitted friends with confidence that they would sense something of God's presence in the midst of his people.

The Festivals became a way of teaching by showing rather than telling. We did not talk about the renewal of worship, we *did* it. People from five to eighty-five, from the most extrovert to the most reserved, could come and sample a freshness of worship where enthusiasm rang through the singing, whether it was 'Our God Reigns' or a Psalm to 'Duke Street'. People discovered that gifts of drama, dance and music had their place, and were encouraged to develop them for themselves.

In the same way, the leadership team spoke volumes to people about the nature of fellowship. It was seen and felt, rather than discussed and explained.

The later attempts to move into another stage of developing people for service were not received so rapturously, but many who wanted to equip themselves for service in prayer, care and sharing were glad to have the opportunity to go deeper than normal congregational life might allow.

The last word must be to say that the value of such events can only be temporary and transient. They are at best models to beckon people forward, signs of something ahead. They are catalysts for change and growth, but they are not ends in themselves. When the catalyst has done its work it is put aside.

The real challenge of such Festivals, if they are true signs of renewal, is to integrate some of the changes into our regular church worship. It is relatively easy to set up an event which is separate, and even seen as an alternative for some, but that is dangerous and sterile. At the end of the day the place for worship, fellowship, teaching, prayer and evangelism is in the local church. Together with other churches, we may be able to share our resources to enable us each to do better what we struggle to do on our own.

If change should come which allows God's glory to be seen more clearly in his Church, it is vital to remember that his glory will only be revealed where there is love. If change should be necessary, let us maintain an attitude of love and patience towards each other during these changes, so that our people may know that they are more important than the changes themselves.

The value of the Festivals of Faith will lie in how far they enable the local churches to be transformed from 'fields in which we are busy, to a force that makes an impact'.

IV
Using Outside Resources

1

Training for Evangelism:
National Resources for Local Mission

St Ninian's, Crieff, serves the Scottish Churches, and the Church of
Scotland in particular, as a Resource Centre for Mission and Renewal.
An understanding of the service it offers requires an appreciation of
the history which has shaped it.

St Ninian's was founded in 1958. The year was significant. In the
warm glow of the post-War years the Kirk in Scotland had made major
advance. The Church had responded to the call of a generation which
yearned to see the old stabilities restored, and a new and better Britain
arising from the ravages of war. In Scotland, at least, that vision was
linked with the Kirk. Through the long years, it had been the Kirk in
the midst of the unrest which had stood guardian of the values of a
Christian society.

That certainly was the dream of National Church Extension as it
planted churches at the heart of the new housing areas which sprang
up throughout the land. The story of that particular chapter in the
record of the Church's mission reads proudly. Reports to the General
Assembly tell of the marvellous encouragement of growing churches
and Sunday Schools which overflowed the modest provision of the
new hall/churches.

Furthermore, returning ex-servicemen of Christian conviction,
many of them preparing to enter into full-time Christian service, held
a vision for Scotland which embraced the whole of the nation's life.
They yearned to see the light of the gospel illuminating the life of the
land, and creating a society in which men and women would seek to
live under the authority of the Lord Christ. They were encouraged on
their way by a Commission of the General Assembly which, during the
dark days of war, had sought to discern God's will for Church and
Nation. With the coming of peace, the clarion call was sounded.

Little encouragement was needed by those who saw the opportunity of these days. Under the leadership of D P Thomson, Evangelist of the Kirk, mission teams travelled the length and breadth of Scotland, harnessing the dedicated energies of many who were seeking to prepare themselves for Christian ministry, along with a formidable body of lay people from all walks of life who responded to the need and the call to Christian witness.

These were stirring days, the more so when it is reckoned that as D P Thomson travelled the length and breadth of the land, George McLeod witnessed his vision of renewal in Church and Nation with the rebuilding of Iona Abbey, and Ronnie Falconer at BBC Scotland astounded the National BBC by mounting a Radio Mission to Scotland which attracted peak listening audiences.

It could only happen in Scotland! The Kirk had a very special place in Scotland's story. At the union of the Crowns, a nation bereft of significant political institutions found its identity in its Church. Through the years, the Kirk had accepted its place of destiny, and had become the champion of a people, jealously guarding their liberty, promoting their welfare, and protecting their rights. So, in this hour the Church of Scotland, with significant title, could claim the place of leadership as Scotland's people sought to move forward towards a new day in the nation's life.

Tell Scotland

It was in such an hour of history that Tell Scotland was born, a movement of mission scarcely paralleled in the record of the years. 'Jesus is Lord', the movement proclaimed, articulating at once the heart of the New Testament witness, the central truth of the many strands of Christian witness, and the Kirk's proud boast down the years, protested fearlessly by Andrew Melville, when, as Moderator of the General Assembly, he defied King James VI. Tell Scotland's proud assertion met the mood of the hour. It took up the echo of history, responded to the deep instincts of people's hopes and dreams, and spurred on a movement of mission which saw the Kirk's communicant membership reaching a new peak of 1.3 million in 1956.

D P Thomson was at the heart of this forward thrust in mission which marked the post-War years. He witnessed a response to the gospel unequalled in all the years of his unrivalled experience. But more, he noted the eagerness of lay people who had responded to equip themselves for Christian work and witness, so that all that had been discovered and experienced during the time of mission might enter into the life of the local church.

So it was that training schools for Christian work and witness became a consistent feature of D P Thomson's campaigns. So it was that a dream was born of some place in the centre of Scotland where people could gather to equip themselves for Christian witness and discipleship that they might lead their churches forward in mission. And this was so in St Ninian's.

Viewed from that perspective, the founding of St Ninian's in 1958 was the culmination of all that had gone before. It carried forward the movement of renewal which centred upon the training and equipping of the ordinary members of the Church, and sought to establish congregations throughout the land as centres of vital Christian witness.

Watershed

That is not, however, the whole story. The year 1958 was a watershed. The growth of the Church which had advanced during the years of hope, peaked in 1956, faltered, and by 1958 had plunged into a gradient of decline which has continued with little remission ever since. That fact is as significant as far as St Ninian's is concerned as all that had gone before.

Tom Allan, the minister of North Kelvinside, a protégé of D P Thomson, and a gifted evangelist in his own right, had been instrumental under God in the emerging of Tell Scotland. In his Glasgow parish, with the help of D P Thomson, he had reached out with the gospel to a population which had grown distant from the Kirk, and had discovered with joy the response that awaited a congregation which sought to embrace its neighbourhood in the love of Christ. The inspiration derived from what happened in that Glasgow parish was foundational for Tell Scotland. There was, however, another side to the story. In the very exercise of reaching out, Allan discovered the forces within the life of the congregation which resisted the initiatives of evangelism and rejected the disturbance of the settled patterns of congregational life. He came increasingly to believe that if there was to be a future for the Missionary Church, it had to be through the 'congregational group', whose commitment gave authentic expression to the gospel at the heart of the church's life. These were the groups which were encouraged in congregations throughout the land. These were the praying people who, with conviction and concern, would carry forward the work of the kingdom.

The times might be ripe for evangelism, but the real question was whether Scotland had a Kirk which could grasp the opportunity. Ronnie Falconer as Religious Programmes Organiser for BBC Scotland experienced a like frustration. His radio mission revealed that throughout Scotland there were many who were simply awaiting the word of invitation. Unhappily, it appeared that frequently there was no great urge to extend it.

So it was that Tell Scotland reached a critical phase in its life. There had always been those whose evangelical convictions decreed that evangelism required the mass event, the star preacher, and the public call to commitment. Tell Scotland had avoided the polarisation which such an event would cause. Its genius had been to draw together the many strands of Christian witness in their common concern to proclaim the Lordship of Christ. But Tom Allan was convinced that an invitation to the American Evangelist, Billy Graham, would provide a new vigour to the movement and give a new focus to the imperative of evangelism. Such was the respect in which Tom Allan was held that many who were distinctly unhappy were prepared to set aside their fears and accept the new situation. Allan's counsel won the day, and the invitation was extended to Graham.

And so the die was cast. The Tell Scotland Crusade packed Glasgow's Kelvin Hall, and the message spread throughout the land. The Graham Team witnessed a response unsurpassed in their experience, and congregations throughout Scotland sallied out in visitation in a climate of heightened interest and awareness of Christian truth.

There are many who still remember these days with warm thankfulness. For many it was the beginning of a Christian commitment which has stayed firm over the years. For many it was the point of calling to Christian service, and many careers of great Christian effectiveness would place their beginning within the context of the Graham Crusade. There are congregations throughout the land where the strains of 'Blessed Assurance'. can still be heard, and memories are cherished of a new spiritual warmth discovered within their fellowship.

It is difficult to accept that these days of massive advance could be followed by disastrous decline. Some, unconvinced from the beginning, simply saw their fears starkly confirmed. Others, among them D P Thomson, reluctantly decided that, with the Crusade, Tell Scotland had taken a wrong turning.

As Thomson painstakingly surveyed the results of the Crusade, he concluded that much of the gain had been more apparent than real. There was little evidence of converts being assimilated within the life of the Church, and more than a little suspicion that the Crusade with its intensive publicity and high personality focus had robbed Tell Scotland of its emphasis upon the central importance of lay witness.

Lessons of Disappointment

Whatever the verdict upon the Tell Scotland Crusade, the foundation of St Ninian's in 1958 gives eloquent testimony to where the Kirk's Evangelists saw the need for the unfolding future. The most urgent task of all in the work of evangelism was building up the lay people of the Church. It was only the arousing of members of the churches to new faithfulness which would carry forward the mission of the Church into every walk of life, and every sphere of human experience.

This, however, was only the beginning. As the ministry of St Ninian's advanced and grew, another agenda developed. Laymen might be inspired to see the need for vital Christian witness. Ministers might be encouraged to develop the missionary parish, but at times only frustration resulted when, as Tom Allan had discovered years before, a congregation was desperately reluctant to adventure in new ways or to accept the call to mission. It was clearly not just people who needed renewal. Structures also needed to be renewed. Churches needed radical re-appraisal if the mission of the Church was to be pursued with vision and effectiveness.

The agenda was widening. The lesson of the changing years was becoming increasingly apparent. No matter how beckoning opportunity might be, if there were not churches vitally responsive to such opportunity, little would avail. It was certainly the painful lesson of the sixties. It was the young people who led the exodus from the churches, soon to be followed by many whose traditional attachment weakened in less congenial times, and latterly by many who became disillusioned and disaffected. Their protest was often expressed as 'Jesus? Yes!—Church? No!'

That protest set the agenda for the Church. It was the signal for the search for relevance. Supremely the Church required to adapt its witness to the circumstances and the issues of a new day, and only a Church which could relate its message relevantly to a changing world could survive. Others, aware of the Church's need to relate to the real world, perceived a parallel need for a real Church. Only a Church which knew its true nature as the Church of Jesus Christ could bear authentic witness. Now that the Church had lost the props of social constraints, it had gained a new opportunity to discover anew its real nature in the purposes of God.

It is against that background that National Resources for Mission must be understood, because resources for mission in the end must reflect what God is teaching his Church regarding its nature and its calling.

St Ninian's as a national resource identifies three distinct areas in its ministry—training, renewal and research.

Training

The foundational principle still stands. Church members eager to increase their effectiveness require training. That training is offered in identified areas of need. It may be training for visitation evangelism, or Christian witness. It may explore the place of music or mime, drama or dance in gospel communication. It may investigate the role of house groups within the life of a congregation. Conferences may be directed towards the specific needs of a particular group: for example, an annual training course for Readers of the Church of Scotland. These events may be organised as courses drawing participation from throughout the land, or they may be geared towards the needs of a particular congregation and address its specific situations and problems. Most training courses occupy the weekend or midweek period, but a year's course is available for those who are able to give this time to 'Training in Evangelism'; and over the course of the year, training is provided during a period of residential study at Crieff with parish placements and mission projects giving extensive experience in a variety of situations.

The prime area for training is identified, however, as related specifically to the eldership. We believe that leadership can only be effective within a congregation which can equip it to fulfil its mission. That, we believe, is the lesson of the past years. It is this area which we identify as of first importance. If the mission of a congregation as it develops and extends is not seen to stem from the prayerful planning of the Kirk Session, but is rather seen as the special concern of a few religious hobbyists, then it is doubtful whether that mission can ever establish itself as central to the congregation's life. A foundational course for Eldership Training is provided which explores the biblical basis, the historical development and the contemporary significance of the eldership, and seeks to establish the Church's need to maintain its life and develop its mission. It is a hopeful sign that these courses are booked to capacity many months ahead.

The foundational course is supplemented by two further courses which are directed towards 'Building Up The Church', and moving towards 'The Missionary Parish'. In the first of these courses the significance of various models of the Church is explored, and their consequences studied as they relate to the 'shape' of a congregation's life. 'The Missionary Parish' takes this a stage further and discusses the ways in which a congregation builds mission into the centre of its life, and relates to the environment within which that mission is to be pursued.

Renewal

Closely allied to the training programme is a conviction that training will in the end avail little if beyond it there is no spiritual motivation which will carry forward the work of evangelism. It is Jesus who is the Evangelist. It is in the power of the Spirit alone that evangelism can be effective. It is, therefore, a prime concern of the ministry of St Ninian's that those who come to learn should be taught of God, and those who seek to equip their churches for mission should know that it is the Spirit alone who equips, and he alone who makes human weakness the vehicle of divine power.

That, of course, introduces an extensive agenda. It reminds us that the truths of the gospel remain remote and restricted until by the power of the Spirit they are transmitted from mind to heart. It reminds us that God's work must be done in God's way, and his gifting through the Spirit is his chosen way to make known his power and his love in the rich variety of his endowment. It reminds us that ministry belongs in God's ordering to all the people of God, and challenges the rooted clericalism of the one-man ministry.

Such an agenda is deeply disturbing. Even when elders and office bearers find new dimensions of understanding, it is often only with difficulty that congregations can move towards new models of functioning. It is because this is so that St Ninian's has developed a ministry of encouragement so that congregations may discover anew their identity, and move towards a deeper appreciation of the mission and ministry which is God's purpose for them in their situation. A Kirk Session weekend conference which brings new realisation and a desire for change can be followed up by a renewal programme within a congregation when the Kirk Session's lead can be backed up by the Field Staff of St Ninian's. Where appropriate St Ninian's is prepared to enter into 'contract' arrangements with congregations whereby, through training events and special projects, a church is encouraged to move forward to become effectively a missionary congregation.

In all of this the St Ninian's youth programme has a special role. It is not only that a weekend conference programme can lead to new dimensions of faith and understanding, but the youth programme,

linked as it is to the enterprise of summer mission, encourages young
people to discover for themselves the adventure of Christian witness
and the challenge of mission. It is in such enterprise that many begin to
understand the meaning of the Church, and the reality of faith. It is
some witness to the importance for young people of this endeavour for
Christ and the gospel that numbers sharing in each summer's programme have been marvellously maintained while other areas of the
Church's youth involvement are sadly depleted. Perhaps there is no
more effective training area than this.

Research
It is of special significance that during the years of decline Church
Growth has become a matter of major interest for the Churches.

It could, of course, be construed as a pragmatic response to decline.
If there are techniques to be learned whereby pews may be filled, then
there could be an obvious interest in acquiring the necessary skills.
This, however, is as unworthy an approach to Church Growth as
evangelism conceived of as a membership recruitment drive.

The truth is that Church Growth becomes an urgent area of enquiry
in any period of church decline, simply because decline calls into
question our convictions regarding the nature of the Church. How
does the promise of Jesus to 'build his Church' relate to the facts of
diminishing membership? Unless we are driven to a 'remnant theology' which encourages us to glory in our smallness, we are bound to look
at the experience of the Church and ask what God is saying to his
people at this moment in their life.

This becomes a matter of paramount importance if we believe that it
is in and through the Church that God wills to fulfil his purposes of
salvation. If it is not God's will that any should perish, then there is
something palpably wrong with a Church which enjoys the cosy
contentment of the 'two or three'. The two or three may, of course,
boast their faithfulness before an unbelieving world, but it is at least
worth considering whether human exclusivism may be as much a factor
in their distance from the world as any principle of Christian faithfulness.

The current problems of the Church amidst a society in the throes of
dramatic social change provide an illuminating example. It is easy to
see the Church's predicament. A secular society is challenging the very
basis of faith, and the Church shrinks within an alien environment. It
is perhaps salutary to be reminded that there is no inbuilt necessity in
the process. The New Testament witnesses to the vitality of a
Christian faith which challenged the pagan world, and mission history

amply illustrates the efficacy of faithful Christian witness during periods of social change. It is when people lose accustomed securities that they can be most open to a faith which helps them to put the pieces together again, and make sense of their lives and their world. The problem of the traditional church is that very often it can be so tied to things as they *were* that it is unable to lead men and women into a future that belongs to God.

That has been the lesson of the years. It is the lesson that is amply illustrated by a Church which sadly often prefers a cherished past to a promised future.

Training for mission depends upon a conviction that salvation is God's will for his world, mission is God's purpose for his people, and growth is God's intention for his Church. On that basis, statistics begin to have a special significance. They are the record of our faithfulness in 'the cure of souls'.

It is part of the ministry of St Ninian's to explore and interpret these 'signs of the times', so that awareness may be heightened within the churches, and pointers be discovered, so that the way of faithfulness may be explored.

Planning for Mission, a study guide prepared by St Ninian's and published by the Department of Ministry and Mission, provides a helpful tool to congregations who are seeking to find ways forward, and St Ninian's field staff are available to assist in the process of enquiry and interpretation. Often it can be in this process of enquiry that new insights are gained, and a missionary leadership is created.

So St Ninian's seeks to provide a service for the Kirk in training, renewal and research. It seeks to be faithful to the lessons of the years, and the insights of its own history.

2

Using a Student Mission Team

'One Monday morning at half past nine the bell rang. Just before we
went in Mr McLennan told us that we were to have a special Bible
lesson and there were four students to give it to us. They came from
the Aberdeen University to teach us about God and his son Jesus.'

So ran the diary of one young pupil in the North of Scotland during a
school visit by a student mission team.

Students! The word provokes different reactions; but this chapter is
concerned with the use of a student mission team in the evangelistic
outreach of the local church.

Each year, usually in the summer or autumn, teams of students are
invited to share in the work of local churches up and down the land.
Each team consists of between 10 and 25 students under experienced
leadership. Members willingly give up part of their holidays and
usually contribute their own financial support to work alongside
church members in evangelism and outreach. They are committed
Christians from different denominations and usually members of
university or college Christian Unions, linked together through the
Universities and Colleges Christian Fellowship.

So why students? Are there any pitfalls? What are the benefits?

Why Students?

The most obvious reason is that students have time available during
the summer and autumn months. But there is another reason. Students can gain a hearing for the Christian message where other more
conventional forms of evangelism cannot. This is not because of any
'intellectual approach'. Students are very ordinary young people; but
some people feel that if the Christian faith can stand up to the
pressures of modern student life, then the views of such people are at

least worth hearing. They also regard them as non-professionals. This is particularly true among young people and young married couples. These are the people whom students reach most naturally and for whom campaigns are specially, but not exclusively, designed to reach. (See the Universities and Colleges Christian Fellowship 'Think Through' Sheet on Local Church Campaigns.)

What are the Pitfalls?

Before the Mission
There are certain pitfalls to be avoided once a congregation has invited a team to work with them. The chief of these involves the attitude of local members to mission and outreach, and their relationship with the team.

A common feature of church life today is the belief that everything should be left to the 'Minister'. An extension of such thinking is to believe that mission should be left to the 'mission team'. It is important, therefore, that a team of students is invited into a situation where adequate preparation has been made. Church members should be informed many months beforehand of the purpose and intention of the mission. A process of education may need to take place on the importance of outreach in the life of a local church. As many members as possible need to be involved in the preparation and planning, as well as in offering hospitality.

In a letter to our own congregation prior to a student mission team visit in September 1984, I wrote: 'They come, not to take over from us, but to share in the work of Christ . . . and to gain experience in Christian service. We give them a warm welcome to our fellowship.'

One very practical way of breaking down any barriers that may exist is to invite the team leaders well before the mission to attend an Annual Business Meeting or a morning service, to introduce themselves and the work that they hope to undertake later in the year.

During the Mission
Assuming that all preparations have been carried out smoothly and the mission is under way, there is a further pitfall to be avoided.

A team of 20 Christian young people working full time with a local church represents a resource that will not be available once the team has departed. It is very tempting during the two weeks of a mission for new areas of work to be opened up within a parish that cannot be adequately staffed afterwards. This is a very frustrating situation and is best avoided by a combination of common sense and forward planning.

Identify the purpose of a two week mission and recognise that although some forms of outreach may be good, they may not be God's will for a congregation at this particular time.

What are the Benefits?

To the Local Church

Over the years experience has proved that a two week visit by a team of enthusiastic and committed Christian students can prove to be a catalyst within a congregation. Many church members have discovered hidden talents that have been brought into effective use. Others on the edge of a congregation have found themselves drawn into the centre.

Dr Jim Packer, commenting on the text 'Go into all the world . . . ' writes: 'Christ's command means that we all should be devoting all our resources of ingenuity and enterprise to the task of making the Gospel known in every possible way to every possible person'. During a student mission every opportunity for ingenuity and enterprise can be taken. Because such a visit breaks the normal routine, churches often find it easier to attempt to break new ground.

Apart from the more usual visitation programme, school visits and speaking at Sunday services, a student team can be invited to run cafés and clubs for teenagers; organise barbecues and film shows; arrange open nights within the congregation; and after-school clubs for children—the possibilities are endless! If successful—then the congregation benefits and is free to continue. If unsuccessful—then they become part of the history of the student team visit!

There can be no doubt that for many active church members the experience of being part of a student mission team has been formative in their commitment to evangelism and wise Christian service in the Church today.

To the Students

Not surprisingly, the greatest benefits from a student mission are experienced by the team members themselves.

For students living away from home and from their local church it is very tempting to make the Christian Union into a substitute church. But this can never be healthy. The student population (and hence the

Christian Union) is not truly representative of society and to turn the Christian Union into a substitute for local church life only removes its members from reality.

The experience of becoming a part of a local church for two weeks and sharing in its work and worship gives a new dimension to the experience of young Christians, who are otherwise caught up in the isolated life of campus.

During a mission, friendships are made that extend beyond the three or four years at university or college. And through such friendships, and acquaintance with the work of a parish different from their own experience, students are often more prepared to seek out situations later in life where they may be best used by God in fruitful evangelism and Christian service.

It has certainly been my own experience that while the benefits of a student mission may appear in the short term to be small, the long term fruit is of great value.

Conclusions

(1) No student mission team by itself will be able to make an impact on a congregation or a parish. It has to be invited to participate in the ongoing work of a local church.

(2) The fruit of this kind of mission activity has to be looked for in the long term—in years, rather than in weeks or months.

3

College Mission Teams

There is a long tradition of student involvement in local church mission. Christian Unions, Student Christian Movements, theological colleges and others have descended on churches during summer or spring vacations and added their enthusiasm to local efforts with a variety of results—usually doing the students a lot of good, more often than not livening up the churches, and often, although not always, being the means for a flow of new folk into Christian fellowship. Is a student team still a worthwhile form of evangelism?

Evidence from Aberdeen

Rather than discussing theoretical issues, this contribution outlines some aspects of recent efforts from Christ's College, Aberdeen, whose students and staff have been working with local churches in the northeast of Scotland: in 1984 at Buckie, a small fishing town on the Banff coast, in 1985 at Montrose, and in 1986 at Elgin. This is a personal account but it is hoped that it will provide sufficient information to encourage others to give some thought to building on the approach adopted, since it seems to the writer that considerably more good than harm resulted from these 'missions' and that much more could be done in Scotland and elsewhere along these lines. This account stresses the many common features, their rationale, and some of the conclusions.

Initiatives came from the College. Three staff and half a dozen students met in 1983 to discuss ways in which a community of theological reflection could act together in mission. This arose in part from the fact that since Christ's College—which belongs to the Church of Scotland—is more or less the same as the Faculty of Divinity of Aberdeen University, but with its own funds, buildings

126

and traditions, the question is constantly raised of the relation between church and theology. Both students and staff are drawn from a variety of denominations and this strengthened an initial conviction that any evangelistic work ought to be as ecumenical as possible. Partly based on Third World experiences but also on local issues, it was strongly felt that the aim of any mission could not be confined to benefiting one parish apart from others around.

In consequence, word was put around among the students that we were thinking of offering to work with groups of churches, and also among the churches that a team was interested in helping in mission. Like some other evangelistic programmes involving outsiders, the time of year had to be limited to Easter or summer vacations, with a preference for the period shortly before a new teaching session started in early October, and the churches had to be willing to provide accommodation and catering facilities. On costs we agreed to suggest that there should be a three-way split between the churches, the team members and Christ's College.

Response from the Churches

We were encouraged by warm invitations which clearly indicated that many people had been looking for help from the theological colleges. Almost all were happy to think along the co-operative lines we suggested rather than a campaign based on one congregation. An important advantage is that it helps to remove suspicion that one church is engaged in 'sheep stealing'. This should be taken seriously since the practice has been observed! It also safeguards against the risk that one minister is bringing in outsiders to cover up a failure to gain the confidence of members as a missionary congregation or, on occasion, a failure to be a good pastor. For all three missions it took time to get a local committee to function, with a working relationship involving one or two members from each church as well as the minister. Such a planning group has a different style from a typical ministers' fraternal method, but the effort involved was felt to be worthwhile not only for the mission but beyond.

Planning

A start was made with a joint meeting in November or December to discuss the feasibility, dates and scope of a joint mission in the area involving the churches and a team from Christ's College. Ideally such a meeting should be held more than a year before the probable dates, ensuring that regular church activities give way to the mission or take it fully into account; something which was never fully achieved in practice. The initial meetings served to relate the expectations and the felt needs of the various churches to the realities of what could be achieved together with a college team.

The two main items were agreed to be: *first,* joint visiting of parts of the area on behalf of all the churches, using pairs made up of one local Christian and one team member, with prior training and preparation; and *second,* new initiatives in youth work, using partly music and drama and concentrating on the younger section of the teenagers unreached by the churches. It was agreed that a series of large special rallies would not be attempted and that 'holiday club' contacts with younger children would not be a major feature. A local committee was set up to liaise with a college committee. The latter appointed specific people to be in charge of working groups on the following aspects of the mission: publicity and literature, visiting plans, youth work, drama and music, Sunday services, accommodation and hospitality, and finance. Other groups varied from year to year and included school programmes, factory visits and children's work.

Regular meetings of the college mission committee were held, with minutes and occasionally a member of the local committee. The local committee also met regularly, often with a couple of representatives from Aberdeen. In addition, on two or three Sundays in the spring, members of the Aberdeen committee took part in church services, with the aim of widening awareness of the proposed mission. A few, but probably not enough, training and discussion meetings were held to draw local people more into the preparation, especially for the visiting programme. As far as accommodating team members was concerned, two church halls were used as dormitories and a third for joint breakfasts and lunches. Evening meals were offered by church members, which proved an excellent way of integrating the team with the local community, but this needs meticulous organisation to avoid mix-ups and is best done by a team member with good local contacts. A couple of families who were happy to provide warm baths and opportunities to 'crash-out' for anyone getting over-tired provided reassurance.

Programme

The timetable followed typical mission patterns with mornings for team preparation, prayer and Bible study, and time to reflect on the previous day's progress. Youth work tends to be open-ended at night and it is harder to get everybody together for long periods then, but an end of the day short service, taken partly by local ministers, for team members who were free and for local people, especially those involved in visiting, seemed to meet a need for many.

For visiting, electoral rolls were used and revised, with information entered on index cards. Care was taken to ensure that where second visits were requested or seemed desirable, the most appropriate minister was given the details the next day. Willingness to visit, not unexpectedly, varied from church to church, but in all cases many people gained confidence and wanted the churches to carry on with a gradual scheme of visiting.

Results

The needs of young people came home to most of the churches, with several people coming forward to do more in the future but with very few churches ready for major changes in their use of time or accommodation. The value of meeting youngsters on neutral ground in a temporary café was confirmed, together with the willingness of many community workers to encourage church involvement in this way.

In all three missions, the problem was highlighted of the concentration of church buildings in one area at a distance from the newer housing, whether public or private, but almost always the churches felt unable to do much about it. Outsiders had to come in on the churches' terms—or so it seemed. This one-sided view of change struck the students forcibly and raised many questions about long-term mission strategy in local churches.

As far as church co-operation was concerned, the positive attitude of many Roman Catholic people and priests was a pleasant surprise for some students and was appreciated by all. Despite the extra work involved and the initial hesitancy of some ministers, the value of working together was clearly recognised by all the students, as was the decisive role of the local ministers, who were often less willing for new ventures than most of their committed members.

There would seem to be far more scope for such missions than has been recognised. Despite the limitations of short-term work, they can strengthen the work and sharpen the vision of the churches and send students back to their studies with a new set of questions and fresh evidence of the reality of the gospel in bringing new life to people.

4

Bible Society Literature for Outreach

Maintaining the Bible at the centre of evangelism is nowadays more complicated than it used to be. There are three reasons for this. *First* of all, the majority of people in our television age are non-book readers. For them, a thick, hardcover volume is a forbidding thing. *Second,* there are today up to ten translations of the Bible in popular use throughout the UK, a variety which has contributed to a widespread loss of the ability to recall the words of Scripture. And *third,* the Bible has become our 'least read best-seller'. According to the Church of Scotland Social Responsibility Department's *Lifestyle Survey* (Quorum Press, Edinburgh, 1987), 69 per cent of Church of Scotland members 'seldom' or 'never' read their Bible, while only a tiny proportion (7.3 per cent) do so every day. Daily Bible reading among Roman Catholics is even lower (4.3 per cent) and, although amongst members of the other Churches it is higher (almost 25 per cent), it must be remembered that they compose only 8 per cent of Scottish Church members.

Nevertheless, there is today a new interest in Christian mission, and records indicate that two Bible versions are being used much more than any of the others in outreach work: these are the Good News Bible and the New International Version. The GNB is the clear market leader overall and one suspects that this is so because of the particular suitability to evangelistic use of its employment of common language.

Common Language and the Good News Bible

'Common language' has been defined as 'the form of language used by fully 75 per cent of people more than 75 per cent of the time' (Eugene A Nida, *Good News for Everyone,* Word Books, Waco, Texas,

1977, p 12). It is also described as 'overlap language' because its range of vocabulary and sentence structure comes from that area in the level of language where literary style and ordinary day-to-day usage overlap. This is in fact essentially the same level of language which the writers of the New Testament employed when they chose the *koine* (common) Greek in preference to the elaborate classical style favoured by most authors of the time.

In addition to employing common language, the GNB was translated on the principle of functional equivalence (meaning for meaning). It thus differs from versions like the Authorised Version and Revised Standard Version which were made on the basis of formal equivalence (word for word), and is able to render technical theological terms like 'justification' by a simple phrase ('put right with God') as well as break down long complicated Pauline sentences into shorter and more easily manageable units. Functional equivalent translation also makes explicit information which is implicit in the original text, but unknown to today's readers. For example, first century Jewish readers knew that the phrase 'Abraham's bosom' in Luke 16:22 referred to the heavenly feast of the righteous—a fact reflected in the Good News Bible rendering: 'to sit beside Abraham at the feast in heaven'.

These basic features of the Good News Bible relate very much to our outreach task today in a society in which the language of theology and even the basic facts of the gospel are largely unknown. While undoubtedly there is a place for formal equivalent translations in close and detailed study of the Bible, it is, I believe, equally clear that the Good News Bible provides us with a unique evangelistic tool because of its common language and functional equivalence. Undoubtedly these two features lie behind its phenomenal sales success world-wide—the New Testament has sold 75 million copies in 20 years and the complete Bible has sold 25 million in 10 years.

Testimonies to the power of this translation abound. A mother of a non-church family in a Scottish new town asked the leader of a church youth organisation that her young teenage daughter was attending: 'What is this book that my daughter doesn't want to put down?' A plumber in Newfoundland was called to repair the pipes in the provincial office of the Canadian Bible Society in St Johns. For a while there was a lot of noise and then, all of a sudden, the pounding stopped and everything was quiet for 30 minutes or so. The Bible Society Secretary wondered what was happening and went down to the stockroom fearing that the plumber had met with an accident. But the man climbed out sheepishly from behind some of the shelves and said, 'Don't worry, I'm not going to charge you for the time'. And then he said, 'You know, I found a Bible there that I can understand and I want to buy several copies of it'.

Evangelistic Use of Bibles

The complete Bible is most commonly used as an instrument of outreach when given as a gift or when used imaginatively in study groups.

There are two editions of the Good News Bible which contain 'helps' for people coming to the Bible for the first time. *The Good News Bible With Introductory Helps* (Bible Societies/Collins, 1986) contains 32 additional pages tinted blue for easy indentification. They include a guide to helpful passages, an overview of the Bible's story, hints for understanding the Bible and a one year reading plan. There is a somewhat similar edition of the NIV with popular helps. The GNB with colour features published under the overall title of *New Life* (BS/Collins, 1987) is specially suited for young people. It contains 80 extra full colour pages interspersed throughout the biblical text and laid out in a 'user friendly' way. These 'helps' are composed of non-controversial factual background information as well as practical hints on subjects like 'Getting started', 'What do we do if we find the Bible boring?' and 'How to study Bible characters'.

Group use of the Bible today—especially among young people—is often more successful if it is linked to some form of activity learning. For example, a group studying Ephesians 2 might produce a poster, or a tape-slide sequence, in an attempt to reproduce the message of the passage in terms which show its relevance to the divisions in today's society. It is surprising how often such attempts to transpose the bibical text into today's situations open up facets of the passage we did not realise were there!

Reference ought to be made at this point to *The Good News Children's Bible*. It contains actual Bible text, not re-written stories. The 330 passages from the Good News Bible are carefully chosen with short introductions to put them into context and to facilitate the understanding of younger children. Where Bible passages are omitted, the introductions also provide the missing links which make the story-line clear. This new Bible has obvious potential in primary schools, Sunday schools and at children's meetings.

New Testaments

New Testaments can be used in many forms of outreach. Chaplains and prison visitors can make them available to prisoners on request. The Gideons distribute them widely to children in the first year of secondary schools. Here again, the version used is at the discretion of the giver, but perhaps *The Good News Colour New Testament* (BS/Collins, 1986) ought to be singled out because its attractive format and its thought-provoking marrying of the biblical text to modern colour visuals help the reader to realise how up to date the Word of God is.

Gospels

The Bible Societies offer several editions of single gospels produced in a variety of formats appropriate to outreach in a non-book reading age. The simplest—the Standard Good News Gospels—can be obtained with special dust-jackets provided by the Bible Society with minimum orders of 1000. These dust-jackets feature a black and white photograph of the distributing church or of a local landmark in order to help the reader make the connection between the gospel and his/her situation. For quantities in excess of 10 000 more substantial localised covers can be provided.

There are also beautifully produced full-colour gospels, available in the GNB and NIV text, and in both A6 (pocket) and A5 sizes. To people brought up in a television age, these gospels are less off-putting than page after page of continuous print.

Scripture Selections

There are many people in our non-reading society for whom even a booklet is difficult to manage, and for them the Bible Societies produce leaflets containing short selections of Scripture. These leaflets are designed to serve as bridges to a gospel or even to the New Testament, and experience shows that habitual non-readers can fairly quickly re-activate latent reading skills once the motivation is kindled.

These full-colour Scripture selections fall into two general categories: counselling and evangelism. The counselling series are addressed to people in situations like bereavement or illness, and are widely used by ministers and elders as they offer hope, comfort and encouragement to people beset by problems. Those designed with evangelism primarily in mind can be used in parish visitation, café outreach, street evangelism and so on. Both types of selection can also be used as the basis for a group Bible study or, indeed, for a formal worship service. When used in church services worshippers should be encouraged to take their copy away, for if read again later it serves as a reminder of the service and as a reinforcement of the sermon or meditation.

Gospels and selections are often most effective when distributed with a word of commendation or in association with a witness event. In this way they become 'tangible tokens' of an act of witness by the individual, congregation or group who distributed them, and will continue to prompt the reader to recall that event and its impact. In this way the message of the selection and the testimony of the event will continue to reinforce one another in the mind of the recipient after the event.

A series of Good News Booklets—obtainable from the National Bible Society of Scotland—containing Scriptures relevant to a particular theme such as 'Marriage' or 'Failure and Success', offer counselling groups a basis for finding solutions in the Word of God to the problems they are confronting. Demonstrating the relevance of the Bible to felt needs often leads to an awareness of the deeper needs of our broken relationship with God.

Bible Use Resources

Some simple Bible use resources with outreach potential are published by the Bible Societies. For example, the 'Beginnings' series of booklets is designed specially for youth groups and the young at heart. The first title—*Just Looking*—presents material for 5 sessions for use in the very early stages of people's interest in Christianity. It enables participants to find out from the Bible what Christians really believe and asks whether it makes sense.

Getting Going is the second title in the series and is designed to help habitual non-readers who are starting to read the Scriptures to overcome young people's prejudices and problems with the Bible. By combining print with graphics, crosswords, word-hunts and other puzzles, *Getting Going* is particularly useful for people who do not belong to the book culture.

Other Bible-use resources include the 'Focus on People' series, designed to help book-shy people relate the experience of famous Old Testament personalities (Abraham, Jacob and Joseph) to their lives today. The 'Steps to Faith' series of 3 booklets, each containing ten basic Bible studies, is also specifically planned to introduce people to the Christian faith. In addition, the 'Connections' series by Jean C Grigor aims to help people form strong, loving, open relationships with each other and to explore what it means to be part of the Christian community.

For a younger audience in a classroom situation the 'Do It Yourself' cartoons are an exciting, creative and practical way to present the Bible to 8–14 year olds. The children are given a sheet of GNB text, with instructions, together with a sheet of cartoon drawings. They listen to the story narrated by Roy Castle on tape and fill in the cartoons with speech and thought bubbles, writing down in their own words what they understand is happening.

A most helpful leadership resource in the area of outreach is *Using the Bible in Evangelism* by Derek Tidball (Bible Societies, 1986). It contains invaluable insights into evangelism as carried out by Jesus and the early Church, as well as offering practical ideas to increase effective evangelism in Bible study groups, on a one-to-one basis, at open-air meetings and in church services.

Postscript

Let me finish by allowing Martin Luther to remind us that the Scriptures are an essential component of evangelism. 'The Bible is alive,' he wrote, 'it speaks to me; it has feet, it runs after me; it has hands, it lays hold on me.'

5

Using a Mission Team

'We need to get more members if the fabric is to be maintained . . . .We need to be stronger if we are not to be united with another congregation when the minister retires . . . .Let's get Stephen Anderson and Scotroc.'

These statements (which have actually been made) express an attitude towards evangelism and mission which can be summed up in two basic assumptions: (a) a mission will get more people into the organisation of our church, and (b) a mission is for a limited period of time and operated by someone from outside.

I have been approached on a number of occasions with a request couched in these terms. When I reply that evangelism must be carried out by the local church, that the principle is about going out to give the gospel rather than to get converts, and that at least a year of prayer and preparation will be required prior to any mission, enthusiasm sadly wanes and the result is generally the 'don't call us, we'll call you' syndrome.

I rejoice that many congregations are beginning to realise that mission must be a part of the ongoing work of the local church, and in such cases I suggest a structure of seven stages:

1 Preparation
The leadership must initially decide on the need for and the format of the mission. Often the nominal leadership will acquiesce while the spiritual leadership takes the initiative. Kirk Sessions are by no means always the initiators, but their support is essential. The next task is to inform the congregation of the plan and to mobilise prayer. In my experience this process of information takes a long time and needs to use every means at our disposal.

2 Teaching
Within the normal framework of the church as a whole there needs to

be a period of specific teaching about the message, motives and methods of mission. At this stage also, a radical reappraisal of structures should be made. Are existing structures suited for their spiritual purpose? Do these structures lend themselves to the growth of new converts? Does the church need to alter its cultural pattern? What are the best ways of helping new enquirers or converts to be built into the church when they come from a totally alien culture as will happen often in Scotland today? How can those who have never expressed themselves in prayer be encouraged to do so? (One church I know had a beginners' group with just four new adult converts who could stammer without embarrassment!) I believe we need to make more use of small groups, perhaps with videos, and encourage interest groups going away together on activity courses and Bible holidays, and other such events. The old minister's enquirers class may have to change to form a bridge from the world into the church.

3 Training

This consists of specific training on personal witness which I have normally led over a period of four weeks with one training class each week. The training is designed to help people 'give a reason for the faith that is in them', and gives practical training for visitation: visits to pubs, schools and so on.

4 Visitation

This involves the visitation of people in their homes (house to house, not door to door!) in the name of Jesus with the gospel. Sometimes people from other churches are enlisted to help, and members of 'Work and Witness' are often involved either in visitation together with local Christians or in the work of house groups which can operate concurrently and so provide the next step into the church. These evangelistic groups—along the lines of Christian tupperware parties— can be the immediate follow-up to a house visit.

5 Outreach

This is a period for reaching out into all areas of the local community. Schools, pubs, community centres, factories and toddler groups are just a few of the areas visited in the past. It is at this stage that members of Scotroc proved of great value although they can never dispense with the necessity of the involvement of the local Christians.

6 Preaching Meetings

This involves a series of meetings to preach the gospel, held in church

F

premises, but with a format more like the culture to which people are used. These meetings are designed to continue the process of bridging the gap between the cultures.

7 Follow-up

The continuing work of helping new enquirers and discipling new converts is an important factor to enable them to join with the church in the ongoing work of the gospel. I am convinced that no church should be content unless converts are not only reproducing the character of Christ but also witnessing for him in the world.

Scotroc unashamedly uses the culture of today in order to communicate the unchanging gospel. We do this on secular ground where modern men and women feel most at home. Paul on Mars Hill adopted exactly the same principle and Scotroc's use of drama is as old as Jeremiah throwing his ruined loincloth at the people of God (Jeremiah 13:1–11) or Ezekiel lying dumb on his side for over a year making sand models of the city of Jerusalem (Ezekiel chs 2–3). Agabus, too, knew the value of the dramatic and visual as he bound Paul with his belt (Acts 21:10–11).

Note that in each case the drama was accompanied by words of explanation—although in the case of Ezekiel the words came later rather than sooner—in marked contrast to Christian drama which, in many instances, relies upon its own veiled communication through method as well as message. We are often told that the performance of certain drama or music can, of itself, communicate saving truth and bring about conversion. Scotroc, being an evangelistic team and not a group for Christian entertainment, recognise that the arts can arouse interest and stimulate thought and questions, but that it is the Word preached that is the agent of rebirth. We recognise that the questions must be answered with words and so preaching forms an integral part of any gospel presentation. Jesus told many parables and yet he had to explain the meaning in words even to his close followers (Matthew 13:1–23).

How is this principle worked out in practice within the framework of a church-based mission as described above?

Scotroc must initially become a part of the local church team. They must meet together well before the mission, pray together and start to enter that relationship which comes from being co-workers with Christ. Scotroc will inevitably take the obvious lead during the outreach phase as they take school assemblies, religious education concerts in schools and pubs, and so on, but always with the prayerful and physical back-up of the local team who can continue personal witness after the performance is over. I remember going to a large pub in the central belt of Scotland and finding a five yard gap along the bar between the Roman Catholics and Protestants. After Scotroc had created considerable stir and the gospel had been clearly presented, the two groups came together round the local Christians who carried on spiritual conversations until ejected at closing time an hour and a half later!

All presentations will include humour and very often some audience participation. The mood will be as varied as the presentation which will include different styles of music, sketches, mime and sometimes tape/slide parables as well as straight-forward preaching. The emphasis is on simple but deep communication.

Seldom do such presentations bring results in direct conversion, although this is by no means unknown. Their greatest impact is to enable people to hear, see and experience the gospel in an environment where they are not automatically closed to the message either by strange surroundings or by the expectations aroused by the church situation. Jesus entered into the hostile environment of this world and engaged in every aspect of its culture. We seek to do the same. He was amongst sinners yet without sin. We seek to enter the sinful realm associated with drama and modern music and yet remain uncontaminated.

The origin of Scotroc lies in the fact that, as the Evangelist of the Church of Scotland, I found I was constantly seeking help in the area of music and drama, and this was often required during the day when employed artists were unobtainable.

A small voluntary team was therefore formed for the period of one year and this pattern has continued to date. Team members are normally aged between 18 and 25 and it is considered right not to expect more than one year of full-time service at that stage in their lives and careers.

Volunteers are strictly briefed that the team is primarily evangelistic and so the spiritual side is of greater importance than the artistic. Nevertheless we are based on the assumption that nothing is too good for the Lord and therefore a degree of professionalism is required. We have suffered for too long in the Church from the amateurism which is shoddy and lazy and indicates an acceptance of standards far below those to be expected from people who serve the Lord Christ. Not all can be brilliant performers, but lack of attention to details such as scripts, timing, props, simple lighting and adequate rehearsal, is inexcusable.

Scotroc members are volunteers who are given hospitality when on missions, and who receive expenses and a small honorarium from a fund grant-aided by the Department of Mission. Many more young people could be used in similar ways. There is a wealth of talent in our churches and many members are unemployed. We should be recruiting such people not just for summer missions, but for long-term missionary teams. Some leadership and equipment would obviously be required, but the cost of setting up, say, four such teams would be less than the cost of three full-time agents. If evangelism is indeed to spread through the Presbyteries then the regional officers appointed are going to need the resources to help missionary-minded congregations. Such teams, recruited and trained for one year, would work with local churches to provide the gifts, zeal and expertise needed to back up the local effort.

As a Church we seem keener to appoint advisers than practitioners. Our rightful stress on the action to be taken at local level can ignore the fact that there are specialist gifts of evangelism which may not be available within every congregation. The 'Scotroc principle' provides a way of making such resources available to the local church in its own environment without excessive cost.

I have become increasingly excited by the way that God has been using Scotroc and long to see a growth in this field, so that we may not merely talk about and plan for evangelism but may actually get involved in reaching out to the people of Scotland in their own communities with the message of the gospel. We have considerable barriers to break down and only the gospel can break through, but it must be presented where people are, and in such a way that people can hear and respond to the grace and call of Jesus.

V
Mission to Young People

1

Young People Outside the Church

The danger of writing a chapter with this title is that it may invite all kinds of generalisations about 'young people today' or even 'the Church today'. Certainly this writer has neither the intention nor the competence to make any such generalisations. Instead, what follows is an account of one particular project which was an attempt at what might be called 'incarnational evangelism' with young people outside the Church. Such a project is unrepeatable. The Spirit of God is far too creative and imaginative for that. But nevertheless observations can be made and lessons learned that might be of help to others. It is with that hope that the following is offered.

Evangelism—as if the Incarnation mattered

First, a word about 'incarnational evangelism'. In considering evangelism it is instructive to begin with an important question: what differences would there be in our approach to evangelism if God had *not* chosen to bring salvation to the world by the way of incarnation? The disturbing truth is that all too often there would be no differences at all. For while we pay lip-service to the glorious truth of the 'Word made flesh', we fail far too often to reflect that truth in our efforts to reach out into the world.

In Jesus, the Son of Man, we see a God who does not confront the world directly, but who first becomes one with humanity, working from within. In the incarnation we see a God who reveals himself by concealing himself, risking his identity in order to share his glory. In the crucified criminal from Nazareth we see not a 'safe' God but One who risked being called a law breaker and a companion of sinners.

Nowhere are these points more crucial than in outreach to young people outwith the Church. The project described here was an attempt at evangelism with young people—as if the incarnation mattered.

143

Cobweb

Cobweb was a late-night coffee bar/music club run by Christians in Aberdeen city centre from May 1979 until May 1984. During that period it went through a number of changes and rode many crises, but when it closed it was probably at its strongest and had reached a fairly stable format.

The aim of Cobweb was to witness Jesus Christ on the world's home-ground; in other words, to take the gospel to people rather than expecting them to come to it. That is very easily said, but much less easily done. A great deal of what passes for 'mission' today is not really mission at all (going to the world) but is an attempt to persuade people to come to us. It was a principle of Cobweb that we had to stand with the world in the world and thus quite deliberately throw aside many of our Christian trappings. Only then could we begin to reach those whom the Church now largely fails to reach, for so often it is precisely the trappings that put people off—particularly young people.

Opening hours
The opening hours for Cobweb were originally Fridays but latterly Saturdays from 11.00 pm to 1.00 am. This was a response to a need—for somewhere for young people to go late at night to meet their friends and enjoy themselves without having to pay extortionate prices. These were very unsociable hours, but why is it that so often the Church has gone to bed just when young people are looking for something to do?

Music
Initially the live music was mainly quiet folk or sometimes ceilidh bands. Memories persist of some bizarre but joyful 'hops' trespassing into the wee small hours. Increasingly, however, in response to demand, we moved towards live rock music featuring local bands and also a good disco. No attempt was made to present Christian or gospel music or to use the music as a direct vehicle for evangelism. We aimed to provide secular entertainment.

Food
Coffee, tea, hamburgers, baked potatoes—all good fare for inebriated punters emerging from the pubs.

Drink
Nothing alcoholic on sale but no restrictions on people bringing in their carry-outs. Evangelism begins with accepting people as they are,

can of lager in hand. To have excluded drink would have meant excluding the people carrying it.

Free Admission

This often came as a pleasant surprise and brought many to our doors who would not otherwise have come. While not vital to the work, free admission did contribute positively to the overall Christian thrust of the club and provided a kind of witness. Latterly a donations system operated with gentle encouragement given to people to pay 50p (cheap by any standards) to help cover costs. This was never forced. Again, to do so might have excluded someone.

The free admission policy was made possible in the early days by using Christian or sympathetic performers who did not demand payment, and latterly by turning the premises into a rehearsal centre for local bands during the week. Large numbers of groups made use of this facility (rehearsal space is much sought after at a time when young music groups are mushrooming) and in return for little or no rent they played at Cobweb for nothing—something many were more than happy to do when opportunities for live gigs were scarce. In this case, as can happen so often, meeting a genuine need among young people turned to our advantage and became a vehicle for aiding evangelism.

The Team

Indispensable to this work was a team of reliable Christians ready to make Cobweb an absolute priority over everything else and to be there every single week—a tall order given the opening hours. We had to learn commitment to each other and to the people who frequented the club. They had to know that they could find any one of us there any week they happened to show up. There was always any number of Christians willing to help when it was convenient, but few willing to give that absolute commitment. Looking back, the fortunes of Cobweb seem often to have depended on the unity, reliability and fellowship of the team. We met together beforehand for prayer, kept up a constant chain of prayer throughout the night and took turns at the various duties involved in running the club.

It is difficult to over-emphasise the kind of commitment involved in long-term projects like this. The Church is often good at hit-and-run missions or crusades that involve great energy and commitment over short periods of time with instantaneous results. What we are less good at is the long-term projects that make much greater demands. As well as speaking of incarnational evangelism, perhaps we should be speaking of covenant evangelism. The God of Jesus Christ is the God of the· covenant—in other words the God of the long-term relationship who is always faithful, always reliable, always there for his people to turn to. Serious evangelistic outreach with young people demands a mentality that reflects God's covenant love. Reliability, faithfulness and solid commitment must be hallmarks of the relationships between workers themselves, and between workers and those they seek to reach.

Witnessing

Our strategy for evangelism was basically to create a secular context and then seek to discover what it meant to be a Christian presence in it. Our identity was often at risk. Many well-meaning Christians would come to investigate and leave, disturbed at what they saw and at what they did not see. Yet the witness was there. The premises were in an increasingly desperate condition, and yet, at its best, despite its very squalid surroundings, Cobweb was a place of celebration in the city centre at an hour when true celebration is hard to find. For Christians to be responsible for that and to be seen participating in it, bopping side by side with the world in the midst of the noise and the mess and the beer cans, was a witness in itself. Of course this was open to misinterpretation but so too was Jesus (see Matthew 11:19).

But obviously it was also a place where opportunities arose in abundance to 'gossip the gospel'. As the team met week by week, we got to know regulars and we learned how to talk to people while serving hamburgers, taking donations at the door, even when queuing for the toilet. Our working model was the incident in John 4:7, where a simple statement, 'Give me a drink of water' (GNB), gave rise to a profound theological discussion that culminated in Jesus' own self-disclosure to an outcast woman. As it became well known that Cobweb was run by Christians, good conversations were initiated more easily.

In addition of course we would meet people outside the club hours wherever possible—going for a drink, inviting them for a meal or to church, visiting them in prison—and several deep and lasting friend- ships were made. Cobweb was not only what happened between the hours of 11.00 and 1.00 on a Saturday night and Sunday morning. It was the starting point for relationships that extended into the week and into our homes, and such relationships are a vital part of evangelism to young people. Trust and credibility have to be earned, and there are no short-cuts.

During the course of the evening there was a centre-spot—the one public, Christian statement in the evening. As the club shifted from a relaxed, laid-back format to a more noisy and boisterous one, this became more difficult, but there was always something said, however brief, to remind people of the Christian basis of the club.

Problems

These abounded! Inevitably we went through violent phases when certain factions and individuals frequented the club and sometimes the police had to be called in. This could be frightening and very upsetting but it had to be seen in perspective, as an occupational hazard. The logic is simple. There is a deep-rooted violence in people which was sometimes on blatant display in those who found their way to our door late on a Saturday night. These people need Christ. Therefore we must risk and accept their violence and try to learn to deal with it, however inadequately. Running away or closing doors achieves nothing.

Vandalism too could be a problem. This was infuriating, and hurtful, but again it had to be seen as an occupational hazard. Real evangelism has its price and it is naïve to think that we can reach those in greatest need without taking risks. We were very fortunate. We had an old disused church hall owned by a sympathetic and understanding church. But how many churches have such facilities? The sad fact is that most churches simply do not have premises that are really suitable for serious evangelistic work with young people. They are designed for meetings, Woman's Guilds and Boys' Brigades. In considering re-building or redevelopment, how much thought is given to the rigours of work with young people outside the Church? Where are our priorities?

Then of course there were drugs, as Cobweb became a place where illegal substances were consumed and sometimes pushed. This caused us heartache and soul-searching. Again, there was the fear of being misinterpreted. Yet drugs are now so widely available that if Cobweb had not been there they would have been no less available. At least at Cobweb there was a chance that those who pushed and used drugs would be challenged by the gospel and shown a better way, and this undoubtedly happened.

Assessing Results

It is always very hard to measure the success of a project like Cobweb. The club went through its good times and its very, very bad times. There were not great numbers converted, but some who now profess faith in Christ would certainly point to Cobweb as contributory. Much of what we were doing was really pre-evangelism—clearing the ground, preparing people for the gospel. Part of our task was to project a different image of Jesus, of Christianity and of the Church which we felt was more accurate: to break down false impressions and caricatures. And that has to be done if we are to reach young people outside our doors.

Christ came to accept us as we are—unconditionally. He told us that he came to bring us life, that we might have it more abundantly. Such acceptance and fullness of life are not evident to many young people in any way that they can relate to when they look at the Church. I would dare to say that something of these could be glimpsed in the bizarre combination of celebration and squalor that was Cobweb at its best, and in the relationships that it spawned. It was a point of contact, a stepping-stone, a place where seeds were sown. Perhaps even a place of incarnation.

The lessons of a project like Cobweb are simple. There are no easy and cost-free ways to reach young people outside the Church. The gap between them and us is yawning and to attempt to bridge it requires commitment, imagination and risk. Until we are ready to offer these, we cannot expect those young people to take us seriously.

2

Young People in Church Circles

The category of young people under consideration here is generally a small proportion of the youngsters in any area. In rural communities or small towns it is often a larger percentage than in inner cities where it might be just a handful of church-goers' children in an area containing thousands of teenagers.

With that depressing or perhaps challenging introduction, it is probably also worth remembering that most growth in youth involvement in the Church starts with these few. After all, the whole Church started with a dozen or so!

A while ago I was bemoaning the fact that 'church-kids' were so conservative. My older and wiser friend said that she thought that they were just more patient. She thought that they tended to be the sort that could see the good and bad sides of the establishment but who were patient with the bad in the hope of what they saw as the possibilities of the good. I think that is right, although I still think that they are conservative, but perhaps because of the same character trait! After all, most churches are clueless when it comes to making young people feel at home. They expect them to dress up, join in with music that they would never choose to listen to, go into draughty, multi-purpose halls for Bible Class, and put up with perpetually superficial relationships with people they only see once a week. This is, of course, nothing new, but it has become exacerbated by the increasingly rapid development of society and youth-culture.

My friend's observation related to another of my own. Church-kids also tend to be more intelligent, or at least more educationally motivated. I put this down to two factors. One is that they might come from similarly motivated families, the other is that most teaching in churches is based around 'concepts' or 'first principles' in Christianity (particularly in non-symbolic Presbyterianism). By this I mean that love, faith, the soul, prayer, and so on, are all taught as themes to be applied, the method of application being left to the interpretation of the listener. This ability to analyse the world around us and refer to basic 'life-concepts' is not common to everyone. A lot of people fail to understand or relate to this type of Christian teaching and will not hang on in with the Church because it has nothing to commend it to them.

What am I saying then? Young people from 15 years upwards in rural areas (12 upwards in cities—to generalise) if they are coming to church and church youth groups, tend to fit into these observations. I say this confidently because I have seen a lot of them, although of course yours might be the exception! 'Church-kids' are not the ones that make a noise down your street at night. In general, they do not go to the local youth club; rather they are likely to socialise with each other during the week, and Sunday is another 'thing' that they do together.

Being aware of this is important in a variety of ways. It is important to realise that we are dealing with a specific cross-section of youth in the parish. It is important because the growth of their faith will involve going beyond their present barriers. It is important because it helps us understand where to begin with the young people in our midst.

Basic Principles

Assume that the young people are sympathetic. Do not apologise for anything that is real to your faith, but instead assume that they agree, and learn how to give them space to disagree. I think that this presumption goes with recognising why they are at your church. I have seen the Christian way unfortunately presented in very defensive terms which can only serve to alienate young people who would be of a mind to agree, except that they are clearly being expected to disagree and will do so despite their own beliefs. This question of attitude is fundamental.

In addition, I think that the decision to be a Christian should be presented to these young people as a daily decision, not a once-in-a-lifetime choice. That does not mean that there cannot be a first day conversion experience for the non-believer, but for many young people in the Church there has never been a day when they did not have some faith in God and it does them a disservice to deny that faith. However, if you present the decision as one of commitment-during-discovery (which it really is for everyone), then the lessons learned in church are part of life, to be applied or denied, and not just theory.

This is especially important with young people who see life in black-and-white terms. I have seen many youth groups become far from Christian in the way that they treat people who have not yet made decisions for Christ.

Activities

In the light of these two principles, what about actual activities in youth groups?

Obviously no form of youth work or education is above the skill of the youth leader. There has been a trend recently to leave the youth of the church to themselves to do 'their thing' and to develop the youth group on their own. I think that this is a mistake. The theory is almost convincing, but in practice groups organised like this do very little, beyond visiting the local swimming pool, inviting the local fire brigade to do a talk and organising a badminton competition! Very few young people in our secular society are confident and competent enough to schedule and develop a group that seriously explores their Christian faith. So do not underestimate the role of a good leader, well supported personally and financially by the church.

The *first* task of the leader is to assess where the group is 'at' in their faith. The *second* is to respond to that with opportunities for discussion and activities that will introduce the next step. For example, a group from a traditional church might never have come across any new forms of worship, or heard somebody's testimony, or talked to a Catholic priest. All three of these simple things could be great eye-openers and bases for the group asking hard questions and taking action. In nearly all the instances that I know of, where people cite moments crucial to the start or growth of their faith, it has been when somebody different related their faith to them. They were made to think afresh and challenged to respond. It is this presentation of information and then challenge which is crucial to development of faith.

This does not have to be by bringing in outsiders all the time. I was once in a youth group that had visiting speakers every week and they all said the same kind of things, because they were basically pro-gramme-fillers who did not know our group at all.

Other group sessions should be designed to help the young people learn and experiment with their faith. This learning comes from discovery, not from didactic methods of teaching. After all, most of our knowledge about life comes this way. Try to create 'open learning experiences'. By this fancy phrase I mean situations in which the group works and learns together. For example, a simulation game which duplicates some kind of real life situation in miniature puts people in set-ups that they are not used to, and they can learn to sympathise with others and look for justice and love in new circumstances. If you do not know what I mean, most development organisations—*eg* Oxfam, Christian Aid—can send you information; or Glasgow Presbytery Youth Office, 260 Bath Street, Glasgow, has a very big selection of simulation games. There are many other possible exercises that can bring real life situations into the midst of your group. Using newspapers is another example. This also helps to make sure that the group are not just theorising about their faith.

Earthing the Teaching

I have a particular aversion to any style of teaching young people that allows them to keep the essence of their faith on spiritual terms. By this I mean that the only way they can describe their faith would be in the realms of metaphysics, using jargon that has no direct relationship to their lifestyle or vocational decisions. It does young people no good to stockpile resources of theology without challenging their daily living in social, economic and political terms. In my old youth fellowship we could quote you everything St Paul said, but we did a quick body-swerve at the Beatitudes! What I am saying is that a *third* and difficult role of the youth leader is not to let young people get away with distancing their faith from themselves by keeping it in the abstract. I am not decrying prayer and Bible study, but we must keep asking, 'What does this mean for us *now*?' Keep the challenge coming and then follow it up. Keep creating the situations and then talk through them. You must expect to put yourself out for these young people continually, otherwise it will be all theory.

Without a doubt situations like summer missions, youth cafés, justice and peace groups, and drama for outreach groups, all make young people grow in their faith, because they are testing themselves and their faith. If you believe that God is their Saviour—and sufficiently—then you will want them to discover it for themselves. It is a test of your faith.

Finally, what about these young people and your congregation? When children reach adolescence it is usually like a bombshell in the family! Similarly, the church congregation as a family cannot get away with shoving the youth out of the congregation because they cause trouble. Their impatience, bluntness, questioning and intolerance of pretence is all part of the wholeness of your church family and they must be part of it in all their honesty. Do not just allow the youth services to let them have their say. That is patronising. Their style and character must be accommodated in your regular meetings. Most ministers have trouble with this and keep going through the old hymn-sandwich routine without consulting their young people. No wonder there are so few young people in the churches. As a youth leader you can find out what they honestly think of their family's worship, take them to other worship situations, find out what they would prefer to have as part of the worship diet for your congregation, and respond to it as is mutually acceptable.

I am now 28. Most of the people that I know who have come to an active faith in the Church now feel there is nowhere to go where they can express their faith in worship. Consequently only about a third of my contemporaries are in active church communion and many have a great struggle with their faith. If you want that to happen to the young people in your church, just keep them out of the organisation of Sunday worship.

G

3
Local Church
Involvement in Summer Missions

Summer Missions have been a feature of the Scottish holiday scene for more years than most care to remember. The experience of the years has shown the value of this work, and in this chapter I hope to highlight the importance of local involvement in Summer Missions, either through welcoming a team to a community or in being part of a resident team elsewhere.

The thinking behind a strategy of Summer Missions is three-fold:

First, Jesus commanded his early disciples to be part of a Missionary Church (Matthew 28:16-20), and what was true for them is true for our generation. The Church ought never to be content to stay within four walls. There must be a consistent desire to reach out and use whatever opportunities are available for sharing the good news of Jesus Christ.

Second, one such opportunity comes during the summer months when people are on holiday—by the seaside, in a caravan park, or at home. People on holiday have time to spare. They are away from the pressures of the normal daily routine, and are much more open to any invitation to a special gathering, or they have time to read a Christian book, or to think seriously about the claims of Christ and his Church.

And *third,* this summer opportunity for evangelism can be grasped by the Church because of the many church folk who are also on holiday during the summer. Younger people, aged 17-30 for example, find the summer mission opportunity particularly exciting, but men and women of every age have a part to play. A task force is therefore available for Summer Mission.

From Seaside Mission to Summer Mission

In a sense, Summer Missions began in the time of Jesus himself. If the traditional model is holiday evangelism on the beach—*ie* Seaside Mission—we remember how Jesus taught and preached by the shores of Lake Galilee. And over the centuries since then, the Christian Church has taken many opportunities for evangelism in the open air.

Summer Mission (then called 'Seaside Mission') became an established part of the work of the Church of Scotland in 1934, through the work of the well-known evangelist, the late D P Thomson. Millport and North Berwick were the two official centres in that year. Every year since then (except for a brief break during the Second World War), Summer Mission teams organised by the national Kirk have been at work in Scotland. In the early years they were concentrated in the traditional seaside resorts, but as holiday patterns changed so did the strategy of Summer Missions. As caravan sites developed in the 1960s, 'Seaside Mission' became known as 'Summer Mission', and teams met with holidaymakers by the side of lochs and in parks. As touring holidays became more popular, so the Church for a time recruited touring Christian literature teams to be in touch with them; as requests from parishes came in for support with summer evangelism for those who stayed at home, so teams were recruited to help congregations with this work as well. And as the holiday patterns of Scotland have changed, so too have Summer Missions—and these changes have served to highlight the significance of the strategy.

The Fruits of Summer Missions

Some might question the value of all this summer activity. They might even argue that, in the normal ordering of life, summer is a time for total relaxation—even among Christians! I have no doubts about both the value and the importance of Summer Mission; and, while I am usually reluctant to write about the results of Christian endeavour, I write now about three results which I have clearly seen:

1 Lives are changed
I am convinced that, whenever and wherever the good news of Jesus Christ is faithfully presented, God through his Holy Spirit challenges individuals to follow the Master in faith. The miracle of conversion takes place. Sometimes the decision to follow Jesus has been taken quietly in a person's heart; sometimes the decision is more apparently dramatic, leading to significant changes in lifestyle and behaviour. I have seen it happen time and time again, and for this I give thanks to God.

2   *People think again about the Church*

Sadly for so many people in Scotland today the 'church' is but the brick or stone building that they pass on their way to and from work. But when people on holiday see a bright, often youthful, team singing modern Christian praise, and presenting the gospel in a new and relevant way, they are sometimes challenged to think again about the Church. Over the years I have come to know many families who have had their thinking about the Church dramatically changed through Summer Mission, and who have found their way back to their local church, there to grow in faith and in service, and for this too I give thanks to God.

3   *What Summer Mission means for those who take part*

So often when Christian people of every age live and work together in the context of Summer Mission, their Christian lives develop immeasurably, with new depths of understanding about fellowship, worship, study, service and evangelism opening up for them. Here I speak primarily of my own experience although it is one which I have witnessed in countless other team members over the years. I volunteered to share in my first Summer Mission while still a senior schoolboy—principally because my parish minister suggested it. My youthful enthusiasm and inexperience must have tested the patience of the team leader! But over that first summer and subsequent summers, I found my Christian life developing and I learned lessons that were invaluable for my winter service in my own parish church. There is no question that in my late teens one of the significant influences in my life, used by God to guide me into the ministry, was the Summer Mission.

Since then I have had an involvement with Summer Mission almost every year. As well as leading many gathered teams drawn from all over Scotland and beyond, I have had the special privilege of taking away teams from my own congregations in Dumfries and Kilmacolm. Like so many others throughout the Summer Mission programme, these teams have returned home to play a special and significant part in congregational life, because of the experience they have gained in the team setting. For this too I give thanks to God.

The results of Summer Mission are clear, and the individuals concerned—those whose lives have been changed, or those who have thought again, or who have shared in the teams—have taken their place in the ongoing work of the Church. There they have made their mark; and there is no question that the Summer Mission strategy over the years has had a significant influence in the whole Church. I have travelled far and wide in Scotland speaking about Summer Missions, and I have yet to address a meeting where someone did not say to me 'I remember . . . ', and then go on to speak about the influence of involvement, or another's involvement, in Summer Missions upon their lives. Summer Mission is an exciting and thoroughly valid strategy.

Getting Involved

Action may take place (A) in one's local situation, or (B) in a team elsewhere.

(A) Every Community has the Potential for Summer Mission Activity

A great opportunity exists to get alongside children and teenagers during the school holidays—and through them to make contact with their parents and families. This chapter cannot give a strategy for every situation but only some guidelines, and enthusiastic encouragement to move forward in your own situation.

Once a local church sees the potential of summer evangelism, the following points need to be considered. The order in which they are discussed is not necessarily significant, since the decisions taken in one area will probably have an effect on the others.

1   Who is going to run the Summer Mission?
Decisions need to be taken at an early stage. There are two choices:

The whole mission is organised and staffed locally: This decision would be taken in the light of the knowledge that there were local people who could effectively lead and staff a mission with the programme envisaged. Remember when considering this option to include every potential helper—of every age and ability. If you are planning a Holiday Club for children, for example, senior citizens may enjoy staffing a Tuck Shop, and a local joiner can often be of valued assistance in making scoreboards and visual aids. Recruiting locally is simplest in terms of accommodation and catering; but make sure the team comes together for prayer and planning beforehand and regularly throughout the mission. Eating together also does much to encourage the fellowship.

A team is invited in: The incoming team could be small or large; whatever the size, it will bring with it certain advantages, particularly freshness. It is vital that from the outset a good working relationship is established with the incoming team, with liaison beforehand, joint participation during, and effective follow-up after, the mission. There is a danger that an incoming team may do more harm than good if they build up effective work over a week or two which is not then followed up by the local church.

With such a team, careful thought has to be given to the following:

Accommodation: Living in homes can help involve local church members in what is happening in the mission, whereas living in the church hall gives team members the chance of greater fellowship.

Catering: If the team are living in homes, some communal meals are beneficial, and some local people should be invited to them from time to time. Or if the team are staying in the halls, donations of baking and other food supplies are always appreciated. Voluntary help with the cooking also builds up good relationships.

Time off: Allow an incoming team time to relax and explore the area. Involve local people in helping them get the most out of their stay. If the team are staying in the church hall, invitations to homes for baths and a soft armchair are always welcome!

2   What is the programme to be?
The possibilities are wide, and could include some—although probably not all—of the following:

A Holiday Club: For children, this could include games (preferably in teams), a Tuck Shop, and a service with choruses, a quiz, and a story. Other possibilities include dividing the children into classes for teaching in greater depth, projects to do at home, a puppet show or a play. Whatever the programme, team members should be encouraged to get to know children individually and to build up relationships with them.

A Teen Time: For younger teenagers—with games, activities, outings, teaching, discussions and music.

A Café: For contacting older teenagers—with music and occasional talks, interviews or drama to help guide conversations. (A word of caution: a café should only be set up if team members are trained and experienced and if the local church is prepared for follow-up.)

Special Services: These could be held at the usual or at different times. Guest preachers, music and drama groups are all possibilities.

Open-Air Work: Including open-air services, street theatre, contacts using survey forms, leaflet distribution or bookstalls in shopping areas.

Family Events: Such as a family night linked to a Holiday Club, or a barbecue in a local park with music, food and evening prayers. This barbecue would be similar to the event described in a beach setting later on.

Visitation: With clearly defined aims, as follows: to give an invitation to the special mission activities, or to the local church; to complete a survey form, using that as a bridge to talk further; and to display and sell Christian literature. At every call, visitors should be encouraged to take every opportunity afforded to share faith.

3 Publicity

Ensure that people know about the events of the mission in good time, and that all will be welcome. Use every publicity channel open to you, including leaflets, posters, the local press and, where possible, local radio.

Backed by faithful preparation and prayer, a Summer Mission in a local community can be a vital strategy for growth in a missionary congregation.

(B) Teams to Lead Summer Mission

Summer Missions are always being requested from elsewhere. These requests often come from the holiday areas of Scotland where local resources cannot meet the missionary opportunities of a large influx of summer visitors, often from large housing areas, with their special needs.

One can be involved in these situations in two ways:

1 As a member of a 'gathered' team drawn from 'all airts an' pairts'

In this type of team one gets to know Christians from a wide range of backgrounds. New friends are made, and faith can grow in the new experience.

2 As a member of a congregational team

When a group from one congregation goes elsewhere to share in the wider mission of the Church, the great advantage is that the team stays together on their return home, and can be effective together over the winter months.

Whatever type of team you join, accommodation is likely to be basic. You will be involved in the full life of the team: Bible study, worship, meal preparation and clearing-up, keeping the billet tidy, and of course in the fun! The programme will be suited to the team and the situation, and training will be offered either centrally or by the team leader. There will be real opportunities for getting alongside people in the holiday setting and for sharing faith.

These opportunities can be illustrated by a visit to a Summer Mission barbecue—typical of many such events organised throughout Scotland each summer.

Imagine a sandy cove at an east coast holiday resort. Publicity has been well distributed by the Summer Mission team, and by 8.00 pm the scene is set for a barbecue. A fire is lit, public address equipment is in place, a large tarpaulin is on the sand for the children, and a sales point set up for hot-dogs, lemonade, crisps and Christian books. The team's guitarists lead the gathering crowd in action songs and soon a holiday atmosphere is built up. At 8.45 pm there is a break for refreshments and soon hundreds of holidaymakers are enjoying their supper in the open-air. More music follows — well-known Christian songs and solo items—and at 9.30 pm, with a beautiful sunset in view, there is a Bible reading, comment, prayer and the singing of 'The Lord's my Shepherd'. Later, before people return to their caravans and boarding houses, they speak to team members *first* about the enjoyment of their evening and *second* of what it has meant to them. Many of them will not have been in church for many a long year, but this evening they have heard the gospel afresh in word and in action.

That is what Summer Mission is all about—using the opportunities of the summer holidays to meet with men and women, girls and boys, and young people; and over the bridge of holiday friendship comes the sharing of the good news of Jesus Christ.

4

Holiday Clubs for Children

A Holiday Club is a programme of outreach to children and their families in the summer months (when Sunday schools do not normally meet) or during the Easter school holidays. It can be organised in any area or community; it is certainly not an activity for holiday resorts alone. The holiday weeks are a good time to get to know neighbours and incomers. It is often in the more relaxed atmosphere of holidays that youngsters and adults have time to think and ask questions. It is also a time when members of a local church, perhaps with some outside help from students or a mission team, can put their faith into practice, and use their talents in the work of evangelism. Holiday Clubs can become regular and vital features in a church's life each year.

Aims

The aims of Holiday Clubs are normally: (a) to reach families for Christ; (b) to provide activities and teaching at appropriate levels to enable individuals to know Jesus Christ as Lord, Saviour and friend; and (c) to encourage personal Bible reading and prayer and growth in Christ.

Most churches plan Holiday Clubs for children chiefly from 7–12 years, but others have provided family activities and events for teenagers and adults as well. The programme must clearly depend on the resources and personnel available. The clubs may be for those who come to church but are equally planned for those who do not.

When?

Summer holidays seem the obvious answer. For some churches this is the best time, particularly the beginning or end of the school holiday period. The value of an August Holiday Club is that the people contacted can be followed up in the church work in the new session immediately after. The school October holiday week can also be a useful time to establish relationships once the session has started. But many people go away in summer, and it can be therefore a difficult time to produce a full team of helpers. For this reason some churches have opted for the Easter holidays when the weather is suitable for outdoor activities and the time of year provides a natural opportunity to focus on the Easter message.

Where?

Church halls may be ideal for the purpose. Some churches have been able to use a local school for their Holiday Club, with its full facilities—a good number of large rooms, chairs, desks, sinks, a kitchen, perhaps a sports hall or swimming pool and games field. A marquee in a central position can add a holiday 'feel' to the club and provide an attractive and useful meeting place—but weather and security need to be considered. Some churches have run a number of small Holiday Club groups in member's homes, which have proved very successful. The warmth and informality of a home can win young people and adults in a way that a large impersonal gathering may not. Those who fear discipline problems in handling large numbers of lively youngsters will find that they do not seem to occur in a House Club group. It is often easier and more natural to discuss Christian things openly in such an environment.

Programme—Length and Content

Most Holiday Clubs last for five or ten days providing activities and teaching each day. In many cases the response to this has been so encouraging that a weekly or monthly club evening has been held thereafter for some weeks, or in some cases throughout the session, to maintain contact. Others feel that it is better to channel new contacts into existing church groups and organisations.

The programme calls for careful planning several months in advance. An overall leader is required and other individuals should be given specific jobs to do. It is worth appointing a leader for each age group, *eg* 5–7 year olds, 7–9, 9–11, 11–13, and so on. Each leader can then plan the activities for his age group with his team of helpers within the framework worked out previously.

It is well worth choosing a theme and building a programme around that. Some excellent material for Holiday Clubs is produced by Scripture Union:

Meet Jesus (7–12 year olds) 14-day programme or 2 × 7-day programmes. Each day looks at a different name of Jesus.

The I Am's of Jesus (7–12) 5-day programme.

People Who Met Jesus (7–12) 10-day programme.

The Jesus Files (11–13) 10-day programme.

The King's Club and *Secret Agents* (5–11) 5-day programme.

All these are useful books with complete Holiday Club programmes covering resources, ideas, teaching, and so on.

Videos and soundstrips such as those mentioned below have been greatly used. Worksheets and activity materials are available with these and may be photocopied. Their value is that each presents a series of stories from one book of the Bible, usually a gospel:

Luke Street—stories of eight houses from Luke's Gospel.

Follow the Leader—based on Matthew's Gospel.

Signposts—seven incidents from John's Gospel.

On Fire—six stories from Acts.

Further help on running a Holiday Club can be obtained from the following books:

Have a Holiday Mission, Margaret Shearer (Scripture Union, London)

Know how to run a Holiday Club, David Savage (Scripture Union, London)

Help Yourself to Work with the 7–13s (National Christian Education Council, Redhill, Surrey)

A Typical Day

Here is a day's programme which has been used successfully by an Edinburgh church's Holiday Club:

9.00 am	Team prayers (time to pray for one another, the children, events). Preparation for children to arrive (essential to be well prepared).
10.00 am	Service (short and simple: several choruses, short Bible reading from Good News Bible, short talk with visual presentation, possibly a memory verse or quiz).
10.30 am	Juice and biscuits.
10.45 am	Craft groups (for example, painting, model-making, frieze work, drama—related to the theme for the day).

11.45 am	Serial story (to be read in parts). You could use, for example, C S Lewis' *The Lion, the Witch and the Wardrobe*. Alternatively this could be a time for 'Keenite groups' to introduce the idea of personal Bible reading. Scripture Union Notes may be helpful for this.
12.00	Lunch and time for the team to be together.
2.00 pm–4.00 pm	Outdoor games, or treasure hunts, or visits (for example, swimming, the Waxworks, Observatory, *etc*).
5.00 pm	Team tea.
6.00–7.30 pm	Indoor games (ideas from youth organisation leaders) and soundstrip or video showing.
7.30 pm	Clear up and prepare for next day.
8.30 pm	Review day's activities. Prayer.

Times are strictly adhered to in order to relieve parents' anxiety, to ensure safety, and to allow time for preparation and rest. A daily programme such as this is demanding but very rewarding. It is worth giving children a printed programme of events and information so that parents know exactly what is happening.

Some Holiday Clubs and missions like to have family events such as a Family Service, Family Barbecue, Family Fun Evening, Family Film Night (the films *Tanglewood Secret* or *Treasure of the Snow* have been used helpfully for this purpose), to which all ages are invited. These provide an opportunity for parents to see what the children have been doing and to take part with them.

It is also possible to have events for adults while the children's activities are under way, *eg* house groups, book parties, a film perhaps, or a coffee club (refreshments, speaker, bookstall), or even a sports group (the Christians In Sport organisation can help here). Some of these ideas can be used with teenagers as well. An evening at a sports centre or a swimming pool provides a good opportunity to get to know any participants. A video such as *The Cross and the Switchblade, Joni* or *The Hiding Place* can stimulate thought and discussion. Riding Light Theatre Company's sketches on video are also excellent for this purpose. Some churches have found helpful ideas from Bob Moffat's

Power Pack (Scripture Union, London, 1983) and from the Serendipity Bible Study and discussion books. Again the range of possibilities for adults and teenagers is endless, but in each particular situation what is best will be determined by the interests, abilities and facilities available.

What Sort of Team?

Some churches look for a whole team to come in from outside, but a home-grown team has obvious advantages. Preparation is made easier because team members already see one another regularly. The church can find a deeper sense of fellowship and growth from its members all working closely together. Follow-up is simplified and continuity can be maintained. One church which has had a very worthwhile summer mission for a number of years invites in one overall leader and two or three key helpers, but provides the remaining 50–60 team members from their own congregation. Other churches have less ambitious programmes and are able to provide 10–12 team members. Some churches can provide a leader and an entire team, but look for training, ideas and materials from outside.

A good team will include all types of experiences and gifts, and will put them to good use. Some young Christians can be greatly helped by working with mature Christians, and by being involved as helpers one year can become capable of taking some responsibility in following years. It is advisable to allow one full-time leader per six children so that the children have one person they really know and can identify with. (Plan for more children than you expect!) Part-time helpers can provide extra help for some activities and outings. Personal Bible reading and prayer and team Bible study and prayer are vital in all that is done. 'Unless the Lord builds the house, those who build it labour in vain' (Psalm 127:1, RSV). The work is his, and in every detail he must be glorified—in relationships, language, presentation of his message, and in genuine love for one another.

God touches lives in different ways. A lady who offered to help in this sort of outreach came to the preparation time, realised there her need of Christ and committed her life to him. A child said to his parents, 'I met Jesus there. Do you know him? Come and meet him!' The parents found themselves in church for the first time in their lives. Two Dads committed their lives to Christ as a result of a Holiday Club in their area. Both are now active elders in their church.

What Happens Afterwards?

God's work continues after the Holiday Club is over—and so does ours as we work with him. Team members have a responsibility for those in their groups, to pray for them by name regularly, to keep in touch, to encourage them in Bible reading prayer, and in Sunday worship. Leaders of Sunday School, Bible Class and Youth Fellowship will want to plan their programmes to welcome newcomers and help young Christians to grow in Christ. Sometimes a monthly club evening or family night can help to keep contact with those who remain on the fringe. Small Bible study groups for children or adults can be of real help to young Christians who need encouragement and a chance to talk about the Christian life.

As we prayerfully consider how to reach families in our area with the love of Christ, let us also remember that God, 'by the power at work within us is able to do far more abundantly than all we ask or think, to him be glory in the church and in Christ Jesus to all generations, for ever and ever' (Ephesians 3:20-21, RSV).

Help of many kinds can be obtained from:

Scripture Union, 21 Rutland Square, Edinburgh EH1 2BB (031-229 8931), or 9 Canal Street, Glasgow G4 0AB (041-332 1162).

Mission to Children's Families: Derek Hobson, 68 Echline Drive, South Queensferry, West Lothian EH30 9XG.

5

Children Within the Church:
An Alternative Approach

How well do we cope with children in our Sunday morning services? Jesus said, 'Suffer the little children to come to me'; yet do we merely suffer their presence? It is only too easy to pinpoint some of the traditional difficulties: the children are removed from the service with indecent haste—perhaps after a children's address from the minister which depends on a subtle connection between an object or a story and the gospel, which may fail to connect with the children's worship. They will then make their way to a Sunday School which in its imaginativeness compares rather badly with day school. Alternatively they may stay in church for the whole of a family service, which may give little more than token recognition to the contribution children have to make to the church's worship.

What follows offers an alternative approach, which seeks to give children a more central place in worship, to do justice to the gifts they bring and to integrate them and their families more fully into the congregation.

Preparing an Offering

In 1 Corinthians 14:26 (GNB) we read, 'When you meet for worship, one person has a hymn, another a teaching, another a revelation from God, another a message in strange tongues, and still another the explanation of what is said'. The principle here is that everyone has a contribution to make to worship, an offering that they bring out of their own resources and abilities. This principle often still operates in Pentecostal denominations where there is opportunity for people to testify, share a portion of Scripture, and contribute a word or two. It is an impoverishment of our Presbyterian tradition that we have not worked out a way of applying this principle to our worship. But is there not perhaps a way that it could be applied in relation to the children?

Let us just imagine for a moment a Sunday morning with a different routine, that attempts to do justice to the children. The actual service of worship begins at 11.00 am and children are encouraged to come earlier at 10.15. The main service will have a theme to it that will be taken up and expounded in the sermon. The children are not going to make an appearance in church itself until 11.15, so there is a full hour to explore that theme with the children in an appropriate way, and in an adjoining hall. In that period the children will be divided into their age groups (probably under 5 years old, 5–8,8–12). They will play some games (many favourite children's games can be easily adapted in such a way that they can be used to introduce a particular lesson or biblical passage). They will at some point sit down and be taught the particular story or lesson for that week. There may be a chorus or two or even a brief time of prayer. And in the remainder of the time, each group will prepare something, an 'offering', that they will bring with them into church, based on the theme they have been exploring. It might be a picture, or a poster with a text suitably decorated by the children, perhaps the text that will be preached in the sermon. It might be a simple drama, or mime, based on the theme for the week. This might involve the children dressing up. It might be a song with actions. It might even involve cooking something. What matters is that each age group has something that they can present in church as an offering— their offering. These can be placed on the Communion Table, or performed in front of the congregation, depending on what they are. Every age group can do something, even the under fives.

The service begins at 11.00 am, without the children and Sunday School teachers. This is a time of preparation and approach. Then at 11.15, perhaps during the singing of a hymn, the children enter. If this has not been done already, the morning's theme is then introduced, and this is followed by each age-group presenting their offering. Where simple drama or something similar is involved this may be light-hearted and even noisy, but children have to be able to worship in ways that are appropriate to them and they are generally less sensitive to formality and decorum than adults. Who is to say which is God's preference? This period of 'children's offerings' will probably last about 15 minutes. It can be ended with a chorus or prayer, after which the children leave.

And then what? The children have had their lesson. They have made their contribution to worship. They now have perhaps 25 minutes during which the sermon is preached and the prayers of intercession are offered. They will be returning to the service for the offering (if it is taken after the sermon) and final hymn. In this time they can play more games, or they can work on a banner for the church. There are any number of ways to fill this time. At its most basic it is akin to their 'break' period at school. One advantage of this routine is that this time during the sermon can be supervised on a rota basis, using different adults each week. This means that the situation does not arise where Sunday School teachers always miss the sermon and most of the service.

Variations on a Theme

This is only a suggested outline. Any number of variations is possible. The important thing is that having the children meet before church gives them time and opportunity to prepare their contribution to the service. Their imagination and creativity can be harnessed in a way that gives them a vital input to worship. Rather than just being talked to in a children's address, they can often help to introduce and open up the theme of the service through their 'offerings'. This approach also gives a unity to the service that is often lacking, particularly when the children's address, Sunday School teaching and sermon are quite unrelated to each other.

One variation on the above arises from a question. If the children meet at 10.15, what do the parents who bring them do before the service? One alternative is for the parents to sit in on and participate in this time with the children, making it a family occasion. They could leave before 11.00 to go into church. Another alternative is to have a time of prayer and Bible study in which the parents could look at the same lesson or passage that the children are exploring, and that will constitute the theme of the service. Again, this would end in time for the start of the service at 11.00 am.

A much simpler version of this approach is to dispense with the time before church, but simply to ensure that in their Sunday School time the children prepare something that they bring with them into church for the last part of the service. They can then still have their 'spot' in the worship. Apart from the fact that we would still have Sunday School teachers missing the bulk of the service, the main problem is time. The advantage of meeting beforehand is that there is a good long period to interact with the children and to explore the theme in a full and imaginative way.

An obvious problem with this approach is that it requires far more preparation than is usual for Sunday School. This is inevitable, but it might make Sunday School far more satisfying, as much for teachers as for children. And surely material could be produced that incorporates this approach and gives ideas. At present Scripture Union's material, *Learning Together*, probably comes closest in terms of having a theme for the service that is explored by the different age-groups, but it unfortunately does not incorporate the principle of children preparing 'offerings' that are brought to church and presented.

Potential for evangelism

The above approach has been described in a hypothetical manner. In fact we have been doing this now in my church in London for almost two years and it has transformed our Sunday School—and our worship. Many children come from the neighbourhood purely voluntarily, although their parents do not attend church. They come because they enjoy Sunday mornings. In many cases contact with these children leads to contact with their parents, with potential for evangelism.

Some adults may disapprove of the children's 'spot' in church. At times it can be boisterous, particularly when hastily rehearsed drama is involved. But is that necessarily a bad thing? Is there no place at all for noise and laughter in church? Of course care has to be taken in deciding what the children are going to do, but we could be far more adventurous in what we allow in worship than most churches are at present. Children's worship must be appropriate to children, expressed in ways that are meaningful and enjoyable to them. And certainly in our case many adults feel that the service benefits enormously from their contribution.

Perhaps some educating needs to be done. Many adults come to church with the attitude that the children should be seen and not heard. With that mentality our worship is impoverished and it is not surprising that we often find it difficult to hold on to our children within the Church and to attract new ones. It is high time we stopped regarding children as 'tomorrow's Church' and started seeing them as a vital ingredient of 'today's Church'.

Jesus' attitude towards children would indicate that their worship is to be valued and affirmed. Our task is to extend to it equal value and affirmation, and to enable it to happen. This is part of the responsibility laid upon us for the evangelising and nurturing of our children.

6

Family Services

Family services are the Sunday morning services when all the ages and organisations of the church are invited to come and to take part. This can happen at the main events of the year: Christmas, Easter, Pentecost and Harvest. Other dates can be added: Mother's Day, Remembrance Sunday, flower festivals, Sunday School prizegiving, or the church anniversary. Services to sum up the Sunday School themes can be added to make the programme a regular monthly or six-weekly feature. A link between the Sunday School teaching programme and the Sunday morning themes for the services is very useful in planning family services.

Well-known hymns which put everyone at ease in an uplifted and happy way can be supplemented by some of the short choruses which children learn at Sunday School. Remaining seated, and with the children leading, people learn and enjoy this form of praise without feeling childish. Apart from singing, there are many other ways that children can take part. Artwork, prepared over the preceding weeks, can decorate the church and illustrate the theme. Posters, mobiles, acetate stained-glass 'windows', models, collages, costumes and overhead projector drawings can all be used. These can be referred to in the service to make the children feel that they have taken part and have helped pass on their own insights into the theme of the service.

Children can bring articles to services which help illustrate a theme with their involvement. Gifts for others at Christmas, harvest produce, or symbols of a parent's employment at Harvest Thanksgiving, flowers for summer festivals, decorated eggs at Easter: these can all be the basis for an impromptu address, based on what is brought. Children can also be given presents to take home from the service to remind them and their families of the theme. Christmas and Easter cards, snowdrops or daffodils, palm-leaf crosses, service folders or lapel stickers: these can all serve as an on-going reminder of the family service.

Teenagers and Adults

Family services should be more than just children's services. It is important to make teenagers feel part of the activity. This can be achieved with music—either through singing or instrumentalists—and another good method of inclusion is through drama. Updated versions of Bible parables which are punchy and humorous create an openness which a subsequent epilogue can respond to with a clear explanation of the theme. Dramatic Bible readings, and monologue or dialogue stories which have to be rehearsed and performed, appeal to the young people who attend Bible Class and the Youth Fellowship.

Adult groups can also be involved. An organisation may have its own choir or drama group which could take part. Bible readings or prayers can be done by representatives or by various voices. A recent meeting of an organisation can be mentioned briefly to illustrate the theme of the service.

I like to sum up the theme and draw all the parts of the service together in an illustrated talk, usually with overhead projector material. This gives a sense of cohesion not just to the service but to the theme that has been followed during the preceding weeks in morning services, and in Sunday School and Bible Class groups.

Mission Opportunities

Family services give an open door to mission opportunities. Parents will come to see their children taking part. Organisation members who are not yet in the worshipping community on Sundays can find these occasions their starting point. Baptisms are often held on family service days. Whether for adults or infants, this is one of the great opportunities to proclaim the gospel of grace. This visible sign of repentance and faith is an illustration of the spoken word appealing for conversion and discipleship.

These services are also an outreach to young people themselves, even as they take part in them. Some of this is groundwork, in creating an enjoyable atmosphere which says 'Church is great', and which breaks down some barriers of feeling lost or out of place or even frightened in a traditional service setting. Making a theme very clear with music, drama, visible sign and illustration is an outreach in itself. It is upon these lasting impressions of a clearly understood and memorable presentation that future life-changing decisions will be made.

Drawbacks and Difficulties

What of the potential problems associated with family services? Let us examine some of them, and see how to anticipate and overcome some difficulties.

Some would doubt if children can remain in church for an hour without becoming irritable and a distraction to the congregation. I have not found this a problem. As long as each item in the service is short, and the whole programme moves along smoothly, their attention is kept. Their involvement also keeps the children from being just spectators.

Some feel that adults will be bored if a family service is all at a child's level of understanding, and that they will 'get nothing out of it'. My experience is that, on these occasions, adults can capture a childlike spirit without feeling childish, and enjoy the simplicity and variety of these services, which makes the 'solid meat' of the other services all the more nourishing because there has been an occasional change from it.

Some may feel that the enjoyment of family services may detract from people's appreciation of normal services of worship, and there may be pressures to conform all worship to the family service style. I have not experienced this pressure, but rather found a greater pleasure in the anticipation of both the special events and the normal preaching-centred worship. Both forms are enhanced by the variety and pattern.

Some members of the Sunday School staff are naturally worried about the pressures placed upon them to bring the children's contributions up to an acceptable standard with all the extra preparation involved, and they are also concerned about the time that is taken away from the normal teaching programme. This problem can be solved partly by bringing in other organisations to take part in the family services, and partly by making the service theme an integral part of the Sunday School teaching programme. An important point to make is that children's parts should not be so elaborate that they require too much rehearsal time. In a programme of many different items, each part should be quite simple.

The value to the outreach of the Church of family services outweighs these potential difficulties. Indeed some existing difficulties can be overcome by them. Many people feel a need for a greater sense of pattern in their ongoing worship. This can be given by thematic preaching, or learning through a part of the Bible. It can also be given through a family service programme which could also incorporate these other approaches.

7

Evangelistic Youth Magazines

One of my first introductions to evangelistic activity was taking part in the Operation Mobilisation literature distribution projects in France, Belgium and Italy. I became convinced that distributing Christian literature had an important part to play in evangelism. It had to be followed up by personal visits to those requesting further information, and required the active support of local churches. That work still goes on in Europe and around the world through Operation Mobilisation's summer teams and two ocean-going ships, 'Logos' and 'Doulos'.

In both my previous church at Methil and my present situation in East Lothian, I have found that a weekly publication giving church news and a record of the Sunday services' teaching is a useful extension to the ministry. Many housebound and interested people know what was preached by receiving the weekly paper. In Methil it was called *Manna*, and in Haddington, Garvald and Morham it is called *In Touch*. These have been produced on offset-litho printing machines which keep down the production time and costs but give good quality reproduction.

It was natural to think of using these facilities in youth work, and to produce evangelistic materials which could communicate the Christian gospel to the majority of children and teeenagers who have no Church connection. The survey conducted by the National Bible Society of Scotland in 1985 showed that only 19 per cent of children in Scotland have any Church connection.

Interest in a publication usually increases when it is produced locally and contains local news. Local 'rags' (as small-town newspapers are often called) can be viable even though they do not have the journalistic standards or printing quality of papers with bigger circulation. The same is true for church publications. A local church magazine will be read with more interest than the nationally produced

Life and Work. School magazines may not be so common now, but where produced, they are read avidly to recognise each budding poet and writer. With this in mind, I started to produce two youth magazines: *Open Case* for secondary school level and *Looking Upward* for primary school. These have proved to be a source of outreach to young people.

Open Case

This is a four page publication produced once every school term and published jointly between the Youth Fellowship and the local Scripture Union group in school. It is distributed with the head teacher's approval by the Youth Fellowship to every pupil in school. It has eight columns which could contain stories of 250 words or a two block or three block cartoon. The contents are usually in the following categorries: Youth Fellowship programme with invitation; Scripture Union programme with invitation; an article on the relationship between science and religion; something on the value of the Bible's teaching on ethics and morality; a message to convey the challenge of the gospel to change life; some practical help for school problems; a seasonal item; an invitation to a youth service or outreach meeting, and of course a place for humour. With this blend, the *Open Case* can inform, challenge, teach, help, interest and entertain.

The outreach value of any evangelistic literature has great potential. There is the personal contact with the distributor, identifying him or her as a contact for further information or discussion. The Youth Fellowship in our case have felt their witness enhanced by the magazine, and their meetings made much more inviting to newcomers. There is the persuasive worth of the reasoning and challenging articles in each term's magazine, succinct and pithy enough to become memorable. It is valuable to enlist the support of the school RE staff in a venture like this. They are usually pleased to have good discussion material in the hands of the pupils that will enliven their own, albeit broader, task of teaching religion in general terms.

It can be a very interesting venture for a Youth Fellowship to be involved in. Either writing original material, or selecting and adapting existing material, can be a good Youth Fellowship's evening programme. Typing, artwork, laying out pages, producing on duplicator, offset litho or photocopier, collating and folding, are all important practical and interesting jobs to do together. Some of the material can then be adapted for future use at youth or family services or school assemblies.

Looking Upward

Again this is a four page, once-a-term publication, prepared jointly by our Sunday School and the local Scripture Union group. It has a wide circulation among children and families of Sunday School, Youth organisations and Scripture Union members. It contains information about these various groups' activities, a message to parents entitled 'Why we do it', listing the aims and methods of the various aspects of Christian youth work, a children's puzzle and activity page, a hobby column with a Christian message application, and a regular letter from our Church mascot toy, 'Westie'—a large-sized West Highland terrier—in which he answers children's questions.

There is not a blanket distribution to all children, as this is not the policy in primary schools. But many children on the fringe of church involvement receive it through organisations, and are brought into Sunday School through it. It is also an outreach to their families as they see that the local church is actively interested in Christian education. The link between Sunday School and primary school Scripture Union is important. Many children make their first contact with Bible learning and reading outwith school class and assembly times through Scripture Union. This 'handmaid of the Church' is one of the great allies in church growth.

Any Sunday School magazine, whether for the existing children or for potential increase, is a good project. Forward plans, policy and aims are made clear if they are to be shared with families and children. The programme of themes for family services and other special events can be made known to give children and parents a greater sense of purpose in Christian education.

We are in a battle to win children's hearts and minds for Jesus Christ. At a time when they can have a great appetite for reading, let us give them Christian reading, and help win them for God.

Epilogue

The Way Ahead

The contents of this book are a parable of the way ahead. From a basic agreement of theological outlook and shared concern, we have an exciting range of methodology. Where our evangelism takes seriously the context of our mission, that variety will always be in evidence. Too often we neglect to analyse our church life in relation to the community in which we are called to serve. Lewis Misselbrook's expertise in this field should be a help to many. The carefully thought-out approaches of Roger Simpson and Dennis Lennon force us to take people where they are and learn to think with them. Here is a relevance which is not the mood of the times, but a response to the real needs and questions of real people. The costly and exhausting work of Lance Stone in Aberdeen's 'Cobweb' project shows us that even when we move out beyond our immediate personal contacts, the only valid context for our evangelism will be where it is seen as an integral part of our caring. For many young people, the issue is not how many bright ideas we can have to keep them amused, but how much we actually care about them. That relationship will be the bridge over which they will meet with Jesus.

Variety of approach is an important element for the way ahead, but even more important is the issue of 'normality'. How can our evangelism become part of the normal structures of our congregational life? David Searle's article on pastoral evangelism gives the minister his starting point. The development of house groups at Wester Hailes has provided the context of caring evangelism. Jock Stein's reflections on worship and evangelism open up issues which deserve consideration and action from all of us. Unless the basic structures of the Church in its worship, fellowship and pastoral care are directed towards the goal of making disciples, evangelism will remain the Cinderella of church life. There will be moments of special activity when Cinderella becomes the princess for a time, but soon the pressure of normal church life puts such things back into the corner. It is this desire to see evangelism built into the structures of the Church which has given rise to the Church of Scotland's initiatives placing new responsibilities on the Presbyteries and giving each congregation the identity of the 'Developed Missionary Parish'.

If this kind of approach to evangelism is to take root in our churches, then there are some basic steps which have to be taken.

1   Prayer

Evangelism is God's idea. It is his work and must be undertaken in his power. There can be no sharing of his life without a secure prayer base in the congregation. It may be few, or it may be many. Without prayer everything will be sterile. The prayer meeting, small prayer groups, prayer triplets, telephone prayer circles, as well as congregational prayer and individual prayer—all are ways of harnessing the prayers of people. It is possible to be a praying church and still not be a missionary church, but it is impossible to be a missionary church without being a praying church.

2   Planning

Evangelism is based on personal relationships. Much of the spontaneous witness of the Christian can never be planned. However, planning is an important factor in evangelism becoming part of the church structure. The leadership body must take responsibility for the direction that the church is heading. It is essential that any analysis and approaches be agreed upon by the leadership body as a whole, or else evangelism becomes that optional occasional extra of the few enthusiasts. It helps the cause of evangelism in the church when a group of gifted and concerned people are given the responsibility of thinking through these plans and submitting them to the church. Leadership groups with a standing committee on mission have already made a structural statement about the importance of mission in the mind of that church.

3   Personnel

Many of the questions surrounding our approach will be determined by the people we have available. There will be people, perhaps only a few, who are gifted in evangelism. There will be others with a concern for evangelism, who will be willing to put their gifts of pastoral care, teaching, music, drama, hospitality and friendship behind the chosen course of evangelistic enterprise. Recognise the gifts and release them for that work. Start small, but start what we can continue.

4 Contacts

Where do we start in our evangelism? Start with the personal relationships which already exist through pastoral care, personal friendships, parents of children in our youth organisations, people who attend church or our organisations but have not yet made any commitment to Christ. In most cases, there is an open door. The people we are called to reach are not far away—they are nearer than we think.

5 Content

What do we say? Philip's encounter with the Ethiopian in the Gaza desert provides a model. Under the guidance of the Holy Spirit, Philip discovered where that man was in his secret pilgrimage, and then beginning from that point, preached Jesus to him. Our content will be Christ-centred and life-related. We will learn where to start by learning first to listen. We will learn when to stop by noticing when the other person has stopped listening!

Often people are willing to read a gospel of Mark or Luke and discuss it individually or in a group. For many people it is their first exposure to the true measure of the Man of Nazareth.

6 Communication

Throughout this book we have been introduced to many different methods of communicating the gospel—the steady exposition of Scripture, the use of literature suitable for the people, discussion groups, overhead projectors, music, drama, lunch-time meetings, lectures, guest services, meals and holiday clubs. To adapt General Booth's famous dictum: 'Why should the Devil have all the good ideas?' The methods we adopt will depend on the situation we have to face—with its opportunities and its limitations. Some people learn better in face-to-face encounter, while others like to read and think on their own. The methods will also depend on your resources and gifts. As one country minister put it: 'You have to build the dyke with the stanes that are to hand'.

7 Context

Where is this communicating going to take place? Once again the answers are varied and different for different people and situations. In many cases the answer lies not in doing different things, but in doing the same things differently. It is a question of thinking 'outsider' or 'seeker' as we go about the normal work.

Worship

How do we welcome people? Do we record their visit and follow it up? How long would it take an outsider to learn the heart of the gospel? Do we on occasion pitch our teaching towards the tentative, seeking enquirer?

Fellowship

How easily does the outsider find a way in? Where would we take him if he wanted to ask more questions? Do we have a running 'welcome group', or an 'enquirers group' or an 'agnostics anonymous' group where he can air his 'heresies without anxiety as he fumbles towards the truth in Jesus?

House Groups

Are there groups with an outward focus rather than an inward concern?

Organisations

Would it be possible for each church organisation to hold at least one annual evangelistic evening to make new contacts with the people for whom that group caters? More fundamentally, would that organisation be able to foster the early beginnings of spiritual search? Do they provide a context in which people can come to know Christ, to grow in Christ and begin to show Christ to others?

It is a useful exercise for each organisation to review its purpose in the light of these questions.

All these places assume that the people we are to reach are sufficiently motivated to come to some church-based activity. Clearly this cannot be assumed of everybody. We may have to consider other options, meeting people in the context where they will feel more comfortable, such as a public lounge, or best of all, in their own homes. Taking a short course on Christian basics to a person in his own home can provide a secure basis of understanding and relationship for that enquirer to begin a more active search.

Everybody is different. For some the anonymity of public worship is desirable, for others it is a barrier. For some a small group is helpful, for others it is threatening. For some the step into a church-based activity is easy, for others it is a threshold that intimidates them. 'By all means to reach some' must be our motto.

8 Counsellor Training

Let us assume that our evangelism is successful! The enquirer has been convicted and convinced. The Holy Spirit is opening his eyes to Christ. He turns to the person sitting next to him in church, or in the group and asks: 'What must I do to become a Christian?'

We need to train suitable people to be able to handle this kind of enquiry. The very act of training will be an act of faith, our way of being prepared for God to act.

Such training can become part of the church's continuing programme of teaching and training. Again it may be one or two in the first instance, but such people will be invaluable as the church breaks through the frontiers of unbelief.

9 Caring for New Christians

So ten people have recently come to Christ. What now? Where do we put them? To put it more specifically, what did we do with the last group of people who became members of our church by profession of faith?

Personal contact should be made immediately by the elder (with appropriate training in this kind of care) or by another partner who can encourage the new Christian and befriend him. Within a few weeks the new Christians should be part of a nurture group to build them and discover their gifts for service. Through this group they will be integrated into the life of the congregation in its worship, fellowship and witness.

10 The Continuing Process

As these new Christians are nurtured and encouraged, they should be given basic training in Christian witness and opportunities to engage in some of the evangelistic outlets that have been described. In this way, every Christian is aware of the call to evangelism, and those who are particularly gifted in this work will emerge in the course of the training.

It may be that as we start with those new Christians who came to faith in the last year and begin to work with them, the process will begin to take shape over the next two years. Building people is a slow process. If Jesus took three years with his disciples, can we afford to take less?

Conclusion

The climate is changing. There is an openness to evangelism in the Church that is looking for the way ahead. Evangelism which is local, personal and pastoral will commend itself to those who live with the harmful caricatures of less personal approaches. If God is preparing his people for a fresh thrust in evangelism in our land, then he is already giving the gifts to accomplish that. They too will be emerging in local congregations if we have the eyes to see them. The key to *how* lies with *who*: *who* will pray, *who* will plan, *who* will have the gifts of sharing, befriending, communicating, counselling, caring, encouraging and many more attributes that will be used to alert men and women to the reality of the living Christ?

We look for that day when, in the prophetic vision of Isaiah, the Spirit is poured out on us like water on a dry and thirsty land, and 'one by one, people will say, "I am the Lord's"' (Isaiah 44:5, GNB).